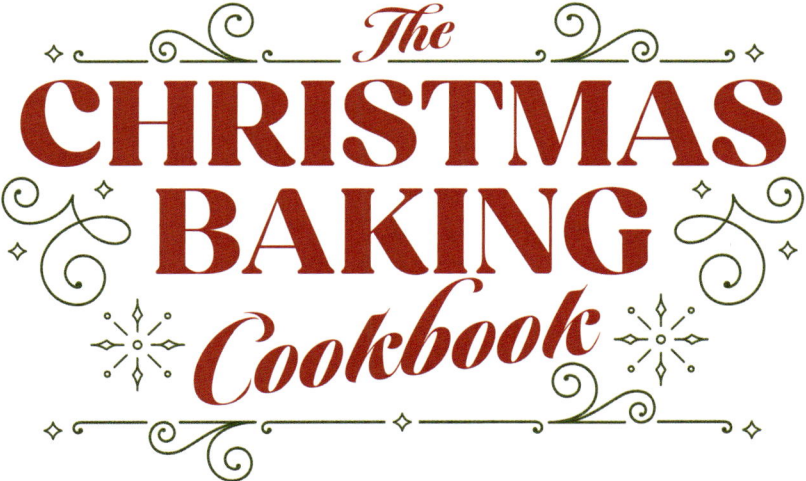

The Christmas Baking Cookbook

Copyright © 2024 by Cider Mill Press Book Publishers LLC.

This is an officially licensed book by Cider Mill Press Book Publishers LLC.

All rights reserved under the Pan-American and International Copyright Conventions.

No part of this book may be reproduced in whole or in part, scanned, photocopied, recorded, distributed in any printed or electronic form, or reproduced in any manner whatsoever, or by any information storage and retrieval system now known or hereafter invented, without express written permission of the publisher, except in the case of brief quotations in critical articles and reviews.

The scanning, uploading, and distribution of this book via the internet or via any other means without permission of the publisher is illegal and punishable by law. Please support authors' rights, and do not participate in or encourage piracy of copyrighted materials.

13-Digit ISBN: 978-1-40034-712-4
10-Digit ISBN: 1-40034-712-2

This book may be ordered by mail from the publisher. Please include $5.99 for postage and handling. Please support your local bookseller first!

Books published by Cider Mill Press Book Publishers are available at special discounts for bulk purchases in the United States by corporations, institutions, and other organizations. For more information, please contact the publisher.

Cider Mill Press Book Publishers
"Where good books are ready for press"
501 Nelson Place
Nashville, Tennessee 37214

cidermillpress.com

Typography: Fields, Tangier

Image Credits: Pages 4, 6–7, 9, 10, 13, 18, 39, 55, 76, 79, 80, 83, 84, 87, 88, 91, 92, 95, 99, 100, 141, 142, 150–151, 167, 168, 171, 179, 202, 205, 206, 209, 226, 233, 234, 237, 250, 253, 254, 257, and 280–281 courtesy of Unsplash. Pages 30, 71, 185, 189, 190, and 210 used under official license from Shutterstock. All other photos used under official license from StockFood.

Printed in Canada

24 25 26 27 28 TC 5 4 3 2 1

First Edition

The CHRISTMAS BAKING Cookbook

'Tis the Season
FOR 100+ FESTIVE TREATS

CIDER MILL PRESS
BOOK PUBLISHERS

Contents

Introduction ◆ 8

Cookies ◆ 11

Cakes ◆ 103

Breads & Breakfast Treats ◆ 143

Pastries ◆ 181

Pies & Tarts ◆ 211

Custards & Other Decadent Confections ◆ 241

Appendix ◆ 263

Index ◆ 283

INTRODUCTION

From turning out hundreds of spritz with Grandma and her magical cookie press to watching Dad spend an entire week patiently preparing pannetone, some of our strongest Christmas memories invariably revolve around the confections that have become embedded in our holiday traditions.

In fact, considering the hold that our favorite holiday desserts have on our minds, it would not be too much to assert that the kitchen is the primary source of the warmth everyone associates with Christmastime.

Since thoughts invariably turn toward sweet treats the minute December rolls around, it makes sense to have as many great recipes for them on hand as possible. Sure, you no doubt have your go-tos. But part of what makes the Christmas season so special is the potential for surprise and the discovery of something new that you can incorporate into your annual celebration. This book provides ample opportunity for both of these to occur, collecting the very best treats from Christmas traditions across the world so that you always shine come Christmastime, no matter what is called for.

Maybe you want to whip up something special with your children or grandchildren as you all take in your favorite Christmas movie. Perhaps you need a new holiday favorite for that friend or loved one who has gone vegan or gluten-free. Maybe you're looking for a treat that will shine on the dessert table at a party.

In the following pages, you will find recipes tailored to these instances and many more. With each new creation, may you put smile after smile on the faces of your loved ones and capture exactly what the Christmas season should be—a time of togetherness and simple pleasures.

You already know that this is the most wonderful time of the year—but you may be surprised how much more wonderful it can be with *The Christmas Baking Cookbook* in hand.

Madeleines, see page 34

Cookies

Among all of the goodies associated with the holidays, none is more treasured than the Christmas cookie. Even Santa Claus, the big man himself, requires plate after plate of them to carry on with his all-important duties.

In keeping with this reality, this chapter is the largest in the book, filled with unassailable recipes for old favorites, and plenty of opportunities to find a new one to incorporate into your tradition.

Classic Gingerbread Cookies

Yield: 24 Cookies ◇ Active Time: 20 Minutes ◇ Total Time: 2 Hours

6 oz. unsalted butter, softened

3½ oz. light brown sugar

⅔ cup molasses

1 large egg, at room temperature

1 teaspoon baking soda

1 teaspoon ground ginger

1 teaspoon apple pie spice

½ teaspoon fine sea salt

½ teaspoon pure vanilla extract

¼ teaspoon freshly ground black pepper

12¾ oz. all-purpose flour, plus more as needed

Royal Icing (see page 264)

Candies, as needed (optional)

1. Place the butter and brown sugar in the work bowl of a stand mixer fitted with the paddle attachment and beat at low speed until combined. Increase the speed to high and beat until the mixture is light and fluffy. Add the molasses, egg, baking soda, ginger, apple pie spice, salt, vanilla, and pepper and beat for 1 minute. Slowly add the flour to the mixture and beat until it is a stiff dough.

2. Divide the dough in half and wrap each half in plastic wrap. Flatten each piece into a disk and chill them in the refrigerator for 1 hour.

3. Preheat the oven to 350°F and line two baking sheets with parchment paper. Place the dough on a flour-dusted work surface and roll it out to a thickness of ¼ inch. Dip cookie cutters in flour and cut the dough into the desired shapes. Transfer the cookies to the baking sheets and place them in the oven.

4. Bake the cookies until they are firm, about 10 minutes. Remove the cookies from oven, let them rest on the sheets for 2 minutes, and then transfer them to wire racks to cool completely.

5. When the cookies have cooled, decorate them with the icing and candies (if desired).

White Christmas Sandwich Cookies

Yield: 20 Cookies ✧ Active Time: 30 Minutes ✧ Total Time: 2 Hours and 15 Minutes

8 oz. unsalted butter, softened

1 lb. sugar

2 eggs

¾ teaspoon pure vanilla extract

9½ oz. all-purpose flour

4½ oz. cocoa powder

1½ teaspoons baking soda

½ teaspoon baking powder

¾ teaspoon kosher salt

1 cup Butterfluff Filling (see page 264)

1 cup white chocolate chips

1. Line two baking sheets with parchment paper. In the work bowl of a stand mixer fitted with the paddle attachment, cream the butter and sugar on medium until the mixture is light and fluffy, about 5 minutes. Scrape down the work bowl with a rubber spatula and beat the mixture for another 5 minutes.

2. Reduce the speed to low, add the eggs one at a time, and beat until incorporated, again scraping the work bowl as needed. When both eggs have been incorporated, scrape down the work bowl, add the vanilla, and beat for another minute.

3. Add the flour, cocoa powder, baking soda, baking powder, and salt and beat on low until the mixture comes together as a dough.

4. Drop 1 oz. portions of the dough on the baking sheets, making sure to leave enough space between them. Place the baking sheets in the refrigerator and let the dough firm up for 1 hour.

5. Preheat the oven to 350°F.

6. Place the cookies in the oven and bake until they are starting to firm up, about 8 minutes.

7. Remove the cookies from the oven, transfer them to a cooling rack, and let them cool for 20 to 30 minutes

8. Place the filling in a piping bag and cut a ½-inch hole in the bag. Pipe about 1 tablespoon of filling on half of the cookies. Use the other halves to assemble the sandwiches.

9. Place the white chocolate chips in a microwave-safe bowl and microwave on medium until they are melted and smooth, removing to stir every 15 seconds. Dredge the sandwich cookies in the melted white chocolate until completely coated and let it set before serving.

Polvorones

Yield: 36 Cookies ◆ Active Time: 20 Minutes ◆ Total Time: 1 Hour

8 oz. unsalted butter, softened

7 oz. confectioners' sugar

4 oz. cake flour, plus more as needed

5 oz. self-rising flour

1 cup almonds, blanched and minced

½ teaspoon pure vanilla extract

Warm water (110°F), as needed

1. Preheat the oven to 350°F and line two baking sheets with parchment paper. Place the butter and 5 oz. of the confectioners' sugar in the work bowl of a stand mixer fitted with the paddle attachment and beat at medium speed until light and fluffy. Add the flours, almonds, and vanilla and beat until the dough is just combined and very stiff. Add a few drops of water, if necessary, to make it pliable.

2. Remove tablespoons of the dough and roll them into balls. Place the balls on the baking sheets and flatten them slightly with the bottom of a glass that has been dipped in flour. Place in oven and bake until lightly browned, about 10 minutes. Remove from oven.

3. Sift the remaining sugar into a shallow bowl and use a spatula to transfer the cookies to the bowl. Roll the cookies in the sugar until they are evenly coated and then transfer them to wire racks to cool completely.

Chewy Ginger Cookies

Yield: 25 Cookies ♦ Active Time: 30 Minutes ♦ Total Time: 2 Hours

6½ oz. unsalted butter, softened

18 oz. sugar

6½ oz. molasses

2 eggs

1½ tablespoons white vinegar

23 oz. all-purpose flour

2 teaspoons baking soda

2 teaspoons ground ginger

1 teaspoon cinnamon

½ teaspoon freshly grated nutmeg

½ teaspoon kosher salt

1. Line two baking sheets with parchment paper. In the work bowl of a stand mixer fitted with the paddle attachment, cream the butter and sugar on medium speed until the mixture is very light and fluffy, about 5 minutes. Scrape down the work bowl and then beat the mixture for another 5 minutes.

2. Reduce the speed to low, add the molasses, and beat to incorporate. Add the eggs one at a time and beat until incorporated, again scraping the work bowl as needed. When both eggs have been incorporated, scrape down the work bowl, add the vinegar, raise the speed to medium, and beat for 1 minute.

3. Add the flour, baking soda, ginger, cinnamon, nutmeg, and salt, reduce the speed to low, and beat until the mixture comes together as a smooth dough.

4. Drop 2 oz. portions of the dough on the baking sheets, making sure to leave enough space between them. Place the baking sheets in the refrigerator and let the dough firm up for 1 hour.

5. Preheat the oven to 350°F.

6. Place the cookies in the oven and bake until lightly golden brown around their edges, 10 to 12 minutes. Do not allow the cookies to become fully brown or they will come out too crispy.

7. Remove the cookies from the oven, transfer them to a cooling rack, and let them cool for 20 to 30 minutes before enjoying.

Cortaditos de Anís

Yield: 20 Cookies ⬥ Active Time: 20 Minutes ⬥ Total Time: 1 Hour and 30 Minutes

- 3 eggs, separated
- 8.8 oz. lard
- 4.4 oz. sugar
- 4 oz. anise liqueur
- Juice of 1 lemon
- 17.6 oz. all-purpose flour, plus more as needed
- 20 blanched almonds
- Confectioners' sugar, for dusting

1. Preheat the oven to 350°F. Line two baking sheets with parchment paper. Place the egg whites in a mixing bowl and beat them with a handheld mixer until they hold soft peaks. Set the egg whites aside.

2. Place the lard and sugar in the work bowl of a stand mixer fitted with the paddle attachment and beat until the mixture is light and fluffy. Add the egg yolks and beat to incorporate.

3. Add the liqueur and lemon juice and beat to incorporate. With the mixer running, gradually add the flour until the mixture comes together as a soft, smooth dough. Add the beaten egg whites and fold to incorporate.

4. Place the dough on a flour-dusted work surface and roll it into a rectangle. Cut the dough into 20 rectangles and place them on the baking sheets. Press an almond into the center of each cookie and place them in the oven.

5. Bake until the cookies are golden brown, 18 to 20 minutes. Remove the cookies from the oven and let them cool on the baking sheets for a few minutes before transferring them to a wire rack. Sprinkle confectioners' sugar over the top and let the cookies cool completely before serving.

Cranberry, Orange & Pistachio Biscotti

Yield: 24 Biscotti ◆ Active Time: 1 Hour ◆ Total Time: 4 Hours and 30 Minutes

4 oz. unsalted butter, softened

Zest of 1 orange

7 oz. sugar

¾ teaspoon pure vanilla extract

2 eggs

10 oz. all-purpose flour

½ teaspoon baking soda

½ teaspoon baking powder

½ teaspoon fine sea salt

4 oz. shelled pistachios, toasted

1 cup dried cranberries

1. Line a baking sheet with parchment paper. In the work bowl of a stand mixer fitted with the paddle attachment, cream the butter, orange zest, sugar, and vanilla extract on medium until the mixture is very light and fluffy, about 5 minutes. Scrape down the work bowl and then beat the mixture for another 5 minutes.

2. Add the eggs one at a time and beat on low until incorporated, again scraping the work bowl as needed. When both eggs have been incorporated, scrape down the work bowl and beat on medium for 1 minute.

3. Add the remaining ingredients, reduce the speed to low, and beat until the mixture comes together as a dough.

4. Place the dough on the baking sheet and form it into a log that is the length of the pan and anywhere from 3 to 4 inches wide. Place the dough in the refrigerator for 1 hour.

5. Preheat the oven to 350°F.

6. Place the biscotti dough in the oven and bake until golden brown and a cake tester comes out clean when inserted into the center, 25 to 30 minutes. Remove the biscotti from the oven, transfer it to a cooling rack, and let it cool completely before chilling in the refrigerator for 2 hours.

7. Preheat the oven to 250°F. Cut the biscotti to the desired size, turn them on their sides, place in the oven, and bake for 10 minutes. Remove from the oven, turn them over, and bake for another 6 minutes. Remove from the oven and let them cool completely before enjoying.

Snowman Cookies

Yield: 16 Cookies ✧ Active Time: 20 Minutes ✧ Total Time: 1 Hour and 30 Minutes

9½ oz. all-purpose flour, plus more as needed

7 oz. unsalted butter, diced

3½ oz. sugar

2 large egg yolks

2 teaspoons pure vanilla extract

Royal Icing (see page 264), as needed

Red candy decorating balls, as needed

Black gel food coloring, as needed

1. Place the flour and butter in a food processor and blitz until the mixture is crumbly. Add the sugar, egg yolks, and vanilla. Pulse until a smooth dough forms, remove it, and form it into a disk. Cover the dough with plastic wrap and chill it in the refrigerator for 1 hour.

2. Preheat the oven to 375°F. Line two baking sheets with parchment paper.

3. Place the dough on a flour-dusted work surface and roll it out until it is ¼ inch thick.

4. Using a snowman-shaped cookie cutter, cut the dough into cookies and place them on the baking sheets. Place them in the oven and bake until the cookies are golden brown and their edges are set.

5. Remove the cookies from the oven and let them cool on the baking sheets for a few minutes before transferring them to wire racks to cool completely.

6. Decorate the cookies with the icing, candy balls, and gel food coloring and let the decorations set before serving.

Pignoli

Yield: 36 Cookies ⋄ Active Time: 15 Minutes ⋄ Total Time: 40 Minutes

1¾ cups unsweetened almond paste

1½ cups confectioners' sugar

2 tablespoons honey

Pinch of cinnamon

Pinch of fine sea salt

2 large egg whites, at room temperature

Zest of 1 lemon

¾ cup pine nuts

1. Preheat the oven to 350°F and line two baking sheets with parchment paper. In the work bowl of a stand mixer fitted with the paddle attachment, beat the almond paste until it is thoroughly broken up. Add the confectioners' sugar and beat the mixture on low until combined.

2. Add the honey, cinnamon, salt, egg whites, and lemon zest, raise the speed to medium, and beat until the mixture is very thick, about 5 minutes.

3. Drop tablespoons of dough onto the prepared baking sheets and gently pat pine nuts into each of the cookies. Place the cookies in the oven and bake until golden brown, 12 to 14 minutes. Remove from the oven and let the cookies cool on the baking sheets.

Vanilla & Matcha Christmas Trees

Yield: 40 Cookies ♦ Active Time: 15 Minutes ♦ Total Time: 1 Hour and 30 Minutes

8 oz. unsalted butter, softened

3½ oz. sugar

1 teaspoon pure vanilla extract

11.3 oz. all-purpose flour, plus more as needed

2 pinches of fine sea salt

1 tablespoon matcha powder

Vanilla Glaze (see page 265)

Candy decorating balls, as needed

1. In the work bowl of a stand mixer fitted with the paddle attachment, cream the butter and sugar on medium speed until the mixture is very light and fluffy, about 5 minutes.

2. Add the vanilla and beat until incorporated. Gradually add the flour, salt, and matcha powder and beat the mixture until it just comes together as a dough. Turn the dough out onto a flour-dusted work surface and gently roll it into a log. Cover the dough with plastic wrap and chill it in the refrigerator for 30 minutes.

3. Preheat the oven to 350°F. Line two large baking sheets with parchment paper. Place the dough on a flour-dusted work surface and roll it out into a ⅛-inch-thick sheet. Using Christmas tree-shaped cookie cutters, cut the sheet into cookies and place them on the baking sheets.

4. Place the cookies in the oven and bake until they are golden brown around the edges, 10 to 12 minutes.

5. Remove the cookies from the oven and let them cool on the sheets for a few minutes before transferring to wire racks to cool completely.

6. When the cookies have cooled, dip one edge into the glaze and sprinkle candy decorating balls over the glaze. Let the glaze set before serving.

Orange Spritz

Yield: 48 Cookies ◇ Active Time: 15 Minutes ◇ Total Time: 45 Minutes

8 oz. unsalted butter, softened

7 oz. sugar

1 tablespoon light brown sugar

Zest of 1 orange

2 egg yolks

9½ oz. all-purpose flour

¼ teaspoon kosher salt

¼ teaspoon baking soda

Confectioners' sugar, for dusting

1 Preheat oven to 350°F and line two baking sheets with parchment paper. Place the butter, sugars, and orange zest in the work bowl of a stand mixer fitted with the paddle attachment and beat until the mixture is pale and fluffy, scraping down the work bowl as needed. Add the egg yolks and beat to combine.

2 Sift the flour, salt, and baking soda into a separate mixing bowl. Gradually add the dry mixture to the butter mixture and work the resulting mixture with your hands until it comes together as a smooth dough.

3 Shape the dough into small logs. Working with 1 at a time, place them in cookie press and press the desired shapes onto the baking sheets.

4 Place the cookies in the oven and bake until their edges start to brown, 10 to 12 minutes.

5 Remove the cookies from the oven and transfer them to wire racks to cool. Dust with confectioners' sugar before serving.

Apricot Kolaches

Yield: 32 Cookies ◇ Active Time: 30 Minutes ◇ Total Time: 2 Hours and 30 Minutes

8 oz. dried apricots

3½ oz. sugar

2.8 oz. all-purpose flour, plus more as needed

¼ teaspoon fine sea salt

2 oz. cream cheese, softened

4 oz. unsalted butter, softened

¼ cup confectioners' sugar, for dusting

1. Place the dried apricots in a saucepan and cover with water. Bring the water to a boil over medium-high heat and cook until the apricots are soft, adding more water if too much evaporates. Add the sugar and reduce the heat so that the mixture simmers. Cook, stirring to dissolve the sugar, until the liquid thickens into a syrup. Transfer the mixture to a blender or a food processor and puree until smooth. Let stand until cool.

2. Sift the flour and salt into a mixing bowl. In the work bowl of a stand mixer fitted with the paddle attachment, beat the cream cheese and butter on high until the mixture is fluffy. Gradually add the dry mixture to the wet mixture and beat to incorporate. Divide the dough into two balls and cover loosely with plastic wrap. Flatten each ball to about ¾ inch thick and refrigerate until the dough is firm, about 2 hours.

3. Preheat the oven to 375°F and line a large baking sheet with parchment paper. Place one of the balls of dough on a flour-dusted work surface and roll it out into a ⅛-inch-thick square. Cut the dough into as many 1½-inch squares as possible.

4. Place approximately 1 teaspoon of the apricot mixture in the center of each square. Gently lift two opposite corners of each square and fold one over the other. Gently press down to seal and transfer to the baking sheet.

5. Place in the oven and bake for 12 to 14 minutes, until the cookies are golden brown. Remove, briefly let them cool on the baking sheet, and transfer to a wire rack to cool completely. Repeat with the remaining ball of dough. When all of the kolaches have been baked and cooled, dust with the confectioners' sugar.

Madeleines

Yield: 30 Madeleines ◆ Active Time: 40 Minutes ◆ Total Time: 3 Hours and 30 Minutes

8 oz. sugar

8 oz. egg whites

Zest of 1 lemon

3.2 oz. fine almond flour

3.2 oz. all-purpose flour

7 oz. unsalted butter

1 teaspoon pure vanilla extract

Confectioners' sugar, for dusting

1 In the work bowl of a stand mixer fitted with the paddle attachment, beat the sugar, egg whites, and lemon zest on medium until the mixture is light and fluffy. Add the almond flour and flour and beat until incorporated. Set the mixture aside.

2 Place the butter in a small saucepan and melt it over low heat.

3 Set the mixer to low speed and slowly pour the melted butter into the mixer. When the butter has been incorporated, add the vanilla and beat until incorporated.

4 Place the madeleine batter mixture into two piping bags. Place the bags in the refrigerator until the batter is set, about 2 hours.

5 Preheat the oven to 350°F.

6 Coat your madeleine pans with nonstick cooking spray. Cut a ½-inch slit in the piping bags and pipe about 1 tablespoon of batter in the center of each seashell mold.

7 Place the pans in the oven and bake until the edges of the madeleines turn golden brown, about 10 minutes. Remove from the oven, turn the cookies immediately out onto a cooling rack, and let them cool completely.

8 Once cool, lightly dust the tops of the madeleines with confectioners' sugar.

Rugelach

Yield: 48 Cookies ◊ Active Time: 1 Hour ◊ Total Time: 2 Hours

For the Dough

8 oz. unsalted butter, softened

8 oz. cream cheese, softened

8½ oz. all-purpose flour

½ teaspoon fine sea salt

For the Filling

1 cup sugar

2 tablespoons cinnamon

½ cup unsalted butter, melted

½ cup finely diced pecans

1. To begin preparations for the dough, place the butter and cream cheese in the work bowl of a stand mixer fitted with the paddle attachment and beat until the mixture is smooth and fluffy.

2. Combine the flour and salt in a mixing bowl. With the mixer running on low, gradually add the flour mixture to the cream cheese mixture until the resulting mixture comes together as a smooth dough. Divide the dough into four pieces, cover them with plastic wrap, and chill them in the refrigerator for 1 hour.

3. Preheat the oven to 350°F. Place 1 piece of dough between two sheets of waxed paper and roll it into a 12-inch circle.

4. To begin preparations for the filling, combine sugar and cinnamon in a bowl. Brush the dough with 1 tablespoon of melted butter, sprinkle 3 tablespoons of cinnamon sugar and 2 tablespoons of pecans over the butter, and cut the round into 12 wedges.

5. Starting at the rounded end, roll up the wedges and place them on parchment-lined baking sheets, leaving 2 inches between them. Curve the ends slightly to give the rugelach a crescent shape.

6. Repeat with the remaining pieces of dough and the ingredients for the filling; you will have some melted butter and cinnamon sugar left over.

7. Place the rugelach in the oven and bake until they are golden brown, about 24 minutes.

8. Remove the cookies from the oven and transfer them to wire racks. Brush the warm cookies with the remaining melted butter and sprinkle the cinnamon sugar over them. Let the cookies cool completely before serving.

Lebkuchen

Yield: 30 Cookies ◇ Active Time: 20 Minutes ◇ Total Time: 1 Hour

1¼ cups hazelnuts, toasted

1 cup almonds, toasted

5¼ oz. sugar

1½ teaspoons cinnamon

½ teaspoon cardamom

½ teaspoon freshly grated nutmeg

Zest of 3 oranges

Zest of 2 lemons

6.4 oz. all-purpose flour

2 tablespoons unsweetened cocoa powder

½ teaspoon kosher salt

3 oz. unsalted butter, softened

5.6 oz. light brown sugar

4 large eggs

1 teaspoon pure vanilla extract

1 cup semisweet chocolate chips (optional)

Vanilla Glaze (optional; see page 265)

1. Preheat the oven to 350°F and line two large baking sheets with parchment paper. Place the hazelnuts, almonds, sugar, cinnamon, cardamom, and nutmeg in a food processor and blitz until the mixture is finely ground. Add the orange zest and lemon zest and pulse to incorporate. Set the mixture aside.

2. Place the flour, cocoa powder, and salt in a small bowl and whisk to combine. Place the butter and brown sugar in the work bowl of a stand mixer fitted with the paddle attachment and cream until pale and fluffy, scraping down the work bowl as needed. Add the eggs and vanilla, reduce speed to low, and beat to incorporate.

3. Gradually add the dry mixture to the wet mixture and beat until the resulting mixture comes together as a smooth dough. Add the finely ground mixture and beat until incorporated.

4. Drop 2-tablespoon portions of the dough onto the baking sheets and place them in the oven. Bake the lebkuchen until the edges are set and the tops start to crack, about 14 minutes, rotating the baking sheets halfway through.

5. Remove the lebkucken from the oven and let them cool on the baking sheets.

6. For chocolate-covered lebkuchen, place the chocolate chips in a microwave safe bowl and microwave on medium until they are melted and smooth, removing to stir every 15 seconds. Dredge the lebkucken in the melted chocolate until completely coated and let it set before serving.

7. For glazed lebkuchen, place the glaze in a bowl. Dredge the lebkuchen in the glaze until completely coated and let it set before serving.

COOKIES

Pepparkakor

Yield: 72 Cookies ✦ Active Time: 20 Minutes ✦ Total Time: 3 Hours

11½ oz. all-purpose flour, plus more as needed

3 oz. almond meal

1 teaspoon cinnamon

1 teaspoon ground cloves

2 teaspoons baking soda

1 teaspoon ground ginger

1 teaspoon cardamom

7 oz. sugar

5.6 oz. brown sugar

8 oz. unsalted butter, chilled and chopped

1 egg

Royal Icing (see page 264)

1. Place the flour, almond meal, cinnamon, cloves, baking soda, ginger, cardamom, sugar, and brown sugar in a mixing bowl and stir to combine. Form a well in the center and place the butter around the well. Place the egg in the well and work the mixture with a pastry blender until it is coarse crumbs. Knead the mixture with your hands until it is a smooth dough. Shape the dough into a ball, cover it with plastic wrap, and chill it in the refrigerator for 2 hours.

2. Preheat the oven to 375°F and line two baking sheets with parchment paper. Place the dough on a flour-dusted work surface and roll it out into a ⅛-inch-thick square. Using Christmas-themed cookie cutters, cut the dough into cookies and place them on the baking sheets.

3. Place the cookies in the oven and bake until the edges start to brown, 6 to 8 minutes. Remove the cookies from the oven and transfer them to wire racks to cool.

4. When the cookies have cooled, place the icing in a piping bag fitted with a fine tip and decorate the cookies with it. Let the icing set for 15 minutes before serving.

Snickerdoodles

Yield: 24 Cookies ◆ Active Time: 25 Minutes ◆ Total Time: 1 Hour

12¾ oz. all-purpose flour

2 teaspoons cream of tartar

1 teaspoon baking soda

2½ teaspoons cinnamon

½ teaspoon kosher salt

8 oz. unsalted butter, softened

11.6 oz. sugar

1 large egg, at room temperature

2 teaspoons pure vanilla extract

1. Preheat the oven to 375°F and line two baking sheets with parchment paper. Whisk the flour, cream of tartar, baking soda, 1½ teaspoons of the cinnamon, and the salt together in a mixing bowl.

2. In the work bowl of a stand mixer fitted with the paddle attachment, cream the butter and all but 2 oz. of the sugar together on medium speed until light and fluffy. Add the egg and vanilla and beat until combined, scraping down the work bowl as needed. With the mixer running on low, add the dry mixture in three increments, waiting until each portion has been incorporated until adding the next. A thick dough will form.

3. Roll 1-tablespoon portions of the dough into balls. Place the remaining cinnamon and sugar in a mixing bowl and stir to combine. Roll the balls in the mixture until coated and place them on the baking sheets.

4. Place in the oven and bake for 10 minutes, until puffy and very soft. Remove from the oven, press down with a spatula to flatten them out, and let cool on the baking sheets for 10 minutes before transferring to a wire rack to cool completely.

Macarons

Yield: 30 Macarons ◆ Active Time: 1 Hour ◆ Total Time: 4 Hours

1. Line two baking sheets with parchment paper. Place the almond flour and confectioners' sugar in a food processor and blitz for about 1 minute, until the mixture is thoroughly combined and has a fine texture. Place the mixture in a mixing bowl, add three of the egg whites and the salt, and stir with a rubber spatula until the mixture is almost a paste. Set the mixture aside.

2. Place the sugar and water in a small saucepan. Place a candy thermometer in the saucepan and cook the mixture over high heat.

3. While the syrup is coming to a boil, place the remaining egg whites in the work bowl of a stand mixer fitted with the whisk attachment and whip on medium until they hold firm peaks.

4. Cook the syrup until it is 245°F. Remove the pan from heat and carefully add the syrup to the whipped egg whites, slowly pouring it down the side of the work bowl. When all of the syrup has been added, whip the mixture until it is glossy, holds stiff peaks, and has cooled slightly. If desired, stir in the food coloring.

5. Add half of the meringue to the almond flour mixture and fold to incorporate. Fold in the remaining meringue. When incorporated, the batter should be smooth, very glossy, and not too runny.

6. Fit a piping bag with a plain tip and fill it with the batter. Pipe evenly sized rounds onto the baking sheets, leaving an inch of space between each one. You want the rounds to be about the size of a silver dollar (approximately 2 inches wide) when you pipe them onto the sheet; they will spread slightly as they sit.

7. Gently tap each sheet pan to smooth the tops of the macarons.

8. Let the macarons sit at room temperature, uncovered, for 1 hour. This allows a skin to form on them.

9. Preheat the oven to 325°F.

10. Place the macarons in the oven and bake for 10 minutes. Rotate the baking sheet and let them bake for another 5 minutes. Turn off the oven, crack the oven door, and let the macarons sit in the oven for 5 minutes.

11. Remove the cookies from the oven and let them sit on a cooling rack for 2 hours. When the macarons are completely cool, fill as desired.

11 oz. fine almond flour

11 oz. confectioners' sugar

8 egg whites, at room temperature

Pinch of fine sea salt

11 oz. sugar

½ cup water

2 drops of gel food coloring (optional)

Mantecados

Yield: 12 Cookies ✧ Active Time: 15 Minutes ✧ Total Time: 1 Hour

4 oz. unsalted butter, softened

¼ cup Spanish extra-virgin olive oil

3½ oz. sugar

Zest of ½ lemon

1 teaspoon fresh lemon juice

1 egg

4¼ oz. all-purpose flour, plus more as needed

¼ teaspoon baking powder

1. Line a baking sheet with parchment paper. In the work bowl of a stand mixer fitted with the paddle attachment, cream the butter and olive oil until light and fluffy. Add the sugar, lemon zest, and lemon juice and beat until pale and creamy, 2 minutes.

2. Add the egg and beat to incorporate. Add the flour and baking powder and beat until the mixture comes together as a dough.

3. Form the mixture into 12 balls and place them on the baking sheet, making sure to leave enough space between them. Press each ball flat with a spatula and chill them in the refrigerator for 15 minutes.

4. Preheat the oven to 375°F.

5. Place the cookies in the oven and bake until they are lightly golden brown, 15 to 20 minutes.

6. Remove the mantecados from the oven and let them cool on the baking sheet for a few minutes before transferring them to wire racks to cool completely.

Florentines

Yield: 30 Cookies ✧ Active Time: 10 Minutes ✧ Total Time: 45 Minutes

5¼ oz. sugar

1 teaspoon pure vanilla extract

7 tablespoons heavy cream

1½ oz. unsalted butter

1½ cups slivered almonds

⅓ cup candied citrus peels

⅓ cup dried cherries or plums, chopped

⅓ cup raisins

1¼ cups dark chocolate chips

1. Preheat the oven to 400°F and line two baking sheets with parchment paper. Place the sugar, vanilla, and cream in a saucepan and bring to a boil. Remove from heat, add the butter, and let it melt. Stir in the almonds, candied citrus peels, dried cherries or plums, and raisins.

2. Place teaspoons of the mixture on the baking sheets, place the Florentines in the oven, and bake until they are golden brown, 5 to 10 minutes, until golden brown.

3. Remove the Florentines from the oven and let them cool on the baking sheets for 5 minutes before transferring to wire racks to cool completely.

4. Fill a saucepan halfway with water and bring to a gentle simmer. Place the chocolate chips in a heatproof bowl, place it over the simmering water, and stir until melted. Spread the melted chocolate on the undersides of the Florentines and let the chocolate set before serving.

Brownies from Scratch

Yield: 12 Brownies ✧ Active Time: 30 Minutes ✧ Total Time: 2 Hours

7½ oz. dark chocolate (55 to 65 percent)

1½ cups unsalted butter

¾ lb. sugar

¾ lb. light brown sugar

¼ cup plus 1 tablespoon cocoa powder

1 teaspoon kosher salt

5 eggs

1½ tablespoons pure vanilla extract

9½ oz. all-purpose flour

American Buttercream (see page 265)

Chocolate shavings, for topping

1. Preheat the oven to 350°F. Line a large round cake pan with parchment paper and coat it with nonstick cooking spray.

2. Fill a small saucepan halfway with water and bring it to a simmer. Place the dark chocolate and butter in a heatproof bowl, place it over the simmering water, and stir until they have melted and been combined. Remove from heat and set aside.

3. In a separate mixing bowl, whisk the sugar, brown sugar, cocoa powder, and salt together, making sure to break up any clumps. Whisk in the eggs, vanilla, and melted chocolate mixture and then gradually add the flour, whisking to thoroughly incorporate before adding the next bit.

4. Pour the batter into the baking pan and use a rubber spatula to even out the top. Lightly tap the baking pan on the counter and remove any air bubbles.

5. Place the brownies in the oven and bake until a cake tester comes out clean, 30 to 40 minutes.

6. Remove from the oven, transfer the brownies to a cooling rack, and let them cool completely.

7. Spread the frosting over the brownies, sprinkle the chocolate shavings over the top, and serve.

Kipferl Biscuits

Yield: 12 Cookies ♦ Active Time: 40 Minutes ♦ Total Time: 2 Hours

6.7 oz. all-purpose flour, plus more as needed

1½ oz. unsweetened cocoa powder

½ teaspoon instant espresso powder

¼ teaspoon fine sea salt

8 oz. unsalted butter, divided into tablespoons and softened

3 oz. confectioners' sugar, sifted

2½ oz. fine almond flour

1 teaspoon pure vanilla extract

½ cup white chocolate chips

1. Place all of the ingredients, except for the white chocolate chips, in the work bowl of a stand mixer fitted with the paddle attachment and beat at medium speed until the mixture comes together as a soft dough. Flatten the dough into a disk, cover it with plastic wrap, and refrigerate for 1 hour.

2. Preheat the oven to 350°F and line two large baking sheets with parchment paper. Remove the dough from the fridge and let it stand at room temperature for 5 minutes. Place the dough on a flour-dusted work surface, roll it into a ¾-inch-thick log, and cut it into 2-inch-long pieces. Roll them to form into cylinders with your hands, while tapering and curling the ends to create crescent shapes. Place them on the baking sheets.

3. Place in the oven and bake for about 15 minutes, until set and firm. Remove from the oven and transfer the cookies to wire racks to cool.

4. Fill a small saucepan halfway with water and bring it to a gentle simmer. Place the white chocolate chips in a heatproof bowl, place it over the simmering water, and stir until melted. Drizzle the melted white chocolate over the cooled biscuits and let it set before serving.

Coconut Macaroons

Yield: 12 Macaroons ✧ Active Time: 45 Minutes ✧ Total Time: 3 Hours

1 (14 oz.) can of sweetened condensed milk

7 oz. sweetened shredded coconut

7 oz. unsweetened shredded coconut

¼ teaspoon kosher salt

½ teaspoon pure vanilla extract

2 egg whites

1. Line a baking sheet with parchment paper. In a mixing bowl, mix the sweetened condensed milk, shredded coconut, salt, and vanilla together with a rubber spatula until combined. Set the mixture aside.

2. In the work bowl of a stand mixer fitted with the whisk attachment, whip the egg whites until they hold stiff peaks. Add the whipped egg whites to the coconut mixture and fold to incorporate.

3. Scoop 2 oz. portions of the mixture onto the baking sheet, making sure to leave enough space between them. Place the baking sheet in the refrigerator and let the dough firm up for 1 hour.

4. Preheat the oven to 350°F.

5. Place the cookies in the oven and bake until they are lightly golden brown, 20 to 25 minutes.

6. Remove the cookies from the oven, transfer them to a cooling rack, and let them cool for 1 hour before serving.

Fiori di Mandilore

Yield: 24 Cookies ⋄ Active Time: 20 Minutes ⋄ Total Time: 2 Hours

4 oz. unsalted butter

6 oz. confectioners' sugar

2 egg whites

1 teaspoon pure vanilla extract

1 teaspoon almond extract

8½ oz. all-purpose flour

½ teaspoon kosher salt

1 egg, beaten

1 cup cherry jam

1. In the work bowl of a stand mixer fitted with the paddle attachment, cream the butter and confectioners' sugar until the mixture is very light and fluffy, about 5 minutes. Scrape down the work bowl and beat for another 5 minutes.

2. Reduce the speed to low, add the egg whites, vanilla, and almond extract gradually, and beat until incorporated. Scrape down the work bowl and beat on medium for 1 minute.

3. Add the flour and salt and beat on low until the mixture comes together as a smooth dough. Transfer it to a piping bag fit with a star tip. Pipe 2-inch-wide roses onto parchment-lined baking sheets, making sure to leave ½ inch between each cookie. Place the baking sheets in the refrigerator for 1 hour.

4. Preheat the oven to 350°F.

5. Gently brush all of the cookies with the egg.

6. Place the jam in a piping bag and cut a ½-inch slit in it. Pipe ½ teaspoon of jam in the center of each cookie.

7. Place the cookies in the oven and bake until the edges are a light golden brown, 15 to 20 minutes.

8. Remove from the oven, transfer the cookies to a wire rack, and let them cool completely before enjoying.

Chocolate & Peppermint Cookies

Yield: 20 Cookies ◊ Active Time: 15 Minutes ◊ Total Time: 1 Hour

4 oz. unsalted butter, softened

5¼ oz. sugar

1 large egg

½ teaspoon pure vanilla extract

¼ teaspoon peppermint extract

5 oz. all-purpose flour, sifted

½ cup cocoa powder

½ teaspoon baking soda

½ cup milk chocolate chips

½ cup dark chocolate chips

Chocolate Ganache (see page 266), warm

Peppermint candies, crushed, for topping

1 Preheat the oven to 350°F. Line two baking sheets with parchment paper.

2 In the work bowl of a stand mixer fitted with the paddle attachment, cream the butter and sugar on medium speed until the mixture is very light and fluffy, about 5 minutes.

3 Add the egg, vanilla, and peppermint and beat until incorporated. Sift the flour, cocoa powder, and baking soda over the mixture and beat until it comes together as a dough. Add the chocolate chips and fold to incorporate.

4 Drop tablespoons of the dough on the baking sheets, making sure to leave enough space between them.

5 Place in the oven and bake until the edges of the cookies are set, 12 to 15 minutes.

6 Remove from the oven and let the cookies cool on the sheets for a few minutes before transferring to a wire rack to cool completely.

7 When the cookies are cool, dip one side into the ganache and sprinkle peppermint candies over the ganache. Let the ganache set before serving.

Alfajores

Yield: 36 Cookies ⋄ Active Time: 1 Hour ⋄ Total Time: 3 Hours

8.9 oz. unsalted butter, softened

5.4 oz. sugar

½ teaspoon kosher salt

1 tablespoon pure vanilla extract

Zest of 1 lemon

4 egg yolks

10.7 oz. cornstarch

7.1 oz. all-purpose flour, plus more as needed

1 teaspoon baking soda

¾ lb. dulce de leche

1 cup shredded coconut

1. In the work bowl of a stand mixer fitted with the paddle attachment, cream the butter, sugar, salt, vanilla, and lemon zest on medium speed until the mixture is very light and fluffy, about 5 minutes. Scrape down the work bowl and then beat the mixture for another 5 minutes.

2. Reduce the speed to low, add the egg yolks, and beat until incorporated. Scrape down the work bowl and beat the mixture for 1 minute on medium.

3. Add the cornstarch, flour, and baking soda, reduce the speed to low, and beat until the mixture comes together as a smooth dough. Form the dough into a ball and then flatten it into a disk. Envelop the dough in plastic wrap and refrigerate for 2 hours.

4. Preheat the oven to 350°F and line two baking sheets with parchment paper.

5. Remove the dough from the refrigerator and let it sit on the counter for 5 minutes.

6. Place the dough on a flour-dusted work surface and roll it out until it is approximately ¼ inch thick. Use a 2-inch ring cutter to cut cookies out of the dough and place them on the baking sheets. Form any scraps into a ball, roll it out, and cut into cookies. If the dough becomes too sticky or warm, place it back in the refrigerator for 15 minutes to firm up.

7. Place the cookies in the oven and bake until lightly golden brown at their edges, about 8 minutes. Remove from the oven, transfer to a wire rack, and let cool for 10 minutes.

8. Place about a teaspoon of dulce de leche on half of the cookies and use the other cookies to assemble the sandwiches, making sure the dulce de leche extends all the way to the edge of the cookie.

9. Place the coconut on a plate, roll edges of the alfajores in it until completely coated, and enjoy.

Kourabiedes

Yield: 40 Cookies ⬥ Active Time: 15 Minutes ⬥ Total Time: 2 Hours

8 oz. unsalted butter, softened

5¼ oz. sugar

1 teaspoon pure vanilla extract

1 tablespoon ouzo

2 large eggs

13 oz. all-purpose flour, plus more as needed

1¼ cups almond flour

Pinch of fine sea salt

3 tablespoons orange blossom water

½ cup confectioners' sugar, for dusting

1 In the work bowl of a stand mixer fitted with the paddle attachment, cream the butter and sugar until the mixture is very light and fluffy, about 5 minutes. Add the vanilla, ouzo, eggs, flours, and salt and beat until the mixture comes together as a rough dough.

2 Turn the dough out onto a flour-dusted work surface and gently knead until it is smooth, about 30 seconds. Divide the dough in half and shape each piece into a log. Cover the dough in plastic wrap and chill it in the refrigerator for 1 hour.

3 Preheat the oven to 400°F. Line two large baking sheets with parchment paper.

4 Cut the dough into 40 pieces and form each one into a slight crescent shape.

5 Arrange the cookies on the baking sheets, making sure to leave enough space in between, and place them in the oven.

6 Bake until the cookies are lightly golden brown and the edges are set, 15 to 20 minutes. Remove the cookies from the oven and let them cool on the baking sheets for a few minutes.

7 Transfer the cookies to wire racks, brush them with the orange blossom water, and dust them with the confectioners' sugar. Let the cookies cool completely before serving.

Pfeffernüsse

Yield: 24 Cookies ◆ Active Time: 30 Minutes ◆ Total Time: 2 Hours

- 11.2 oz. all-purpose flour, sifted
- ½ teaspoon fine sea salt
- ½ teaspoon black pepper
- ½ teaspoon cinnamon
- ¼ teaspoon baking soda
- ¼ teaspoon allspice
- ¼ teaspoon freshly grated nutmeg
- Pinch of ground cloves
- 4 oz. unsalted butter, softened
- 7 oz. light brown sugar
- 3 tablespoons molasses, warmed
- 1 large egg
- 2¼ cups confectioners' sugar

1. Place the flour, salt, pepper, cinnamon, baking soda, allspice, nutmeg, and cloves in a large mixing bowl and whisk to combine.

2. Place the butter, brown sugar, and molasses in the work bowl of a stand mixer fitted with the paddle attachment and beat at medium speed until pale and fluffy, scraping down the sides of the bowl as needed.

3. Add the egg and beat to incorporate. With the mixer running on low speed, gradually add the dry mixture to the wet mixture and beat until the resulting mixture comes together as a dough. Cover the dough in plastic wrap and chill it in the refrigerator for 1 hour.

4. Preheat the oven to 350°F and line two baking sheets with parchment paper. Form tablespoons of the dough into rounded rectangles and place them on the baking sheets. Place the cookies in the oven and bake until the cookies are firm, 12 to 14 minutes.

5. Remove the cookies from the oven and transfer to wire racks to cool briefly.

6. Place the confectioners' sugar in a bowl and toss the warm cookies in it until they are completely coated. Place the cookies back on the wire racks to cool completely.

Goro Cookies

Yield: 24 Cookies ⋄ Active Time: 45 Minutes ⋄ Total Time: 3 Hours

5 oz. heavy cream

1 egg, separated

4.4 oz. sugar

11.4 oz. unsalted butter

5.3 oz. all-purpose flour, plus more as needed

¼ teaspoon cardamom

½ teaspoon pure vanilla extract

1. Using a handheld mixer, whip the cream until it holds soft peaks.

2. Place the egg white and sugar in the work bowl of a stand mixer fitted with the whisk attachment and whip until the mixture holds soft peaks. Add the meringue to the whipped cream and fold to combine.

3. Place the butter, flour, cardamom, vanilla, and egg yolk in a food processor and pulse to combine. Add the mixture to the whipped cream mixture, fit the stand mixer with the paddle attachment, and beat until the resulting mixture comes together as a smooth dough. Divide the dough in half, cover each piece with plastic wrap, and chill the dough in the refrigerator for 2 hours.

4. Remove 1 piece of dough from the refrigerator, place it on a flour-dusted work surface, and roll it into a 1/16-inch-thick rectangle. Cut the sheet to fit a goro iron.

5. Coat the goro iron with nonstick cooking spray and warm it over medium-high heat. Add the dough to the goro iron and cook until the cookies are a light golden brown, 2 to 4 minutes, turning the iron every 20 seconds or so to ensure even cooking.

6. Remove the goro from the iron and cut them into the desired shapes and sizes. Transfer them to a wire rack and let them cool completely before serving.

7. Repeat Steps 4, 5, and 6 with the remaining piece of dough.

Chocolate Chip Cookies

Yield: 16 Cookies ◆ Active Time: 15 Minutes ◆ Total Time: 45 Minutes

7 oz. unsalted butter

8¾ oz. all-purpose flour

½ teaspoon baking soda

3½ oz. sugar

5.3 oz. dark brown sugar

1 teaspoon fine sea salt

2 teaspoons pure vanilla extract

1 large egg

1 large egg yolk

1¼ cups semisweet chocolate chips

1. Preheat the oven to 350°F. Place the butter in a saucepan and cook over medium-high heat until it is starting to brown and give off a nutty aroma (let your nose guide you here, making sure you frequently waft the steam toward you). Transfer to a heatproof mixing bowl.

2. Place the flour and baking soda in a bowl and whisk until combined.

3. Add the sugars, salt, and vanilla to the bowl containing the melted butter and whisk until combined. Add the egg and egg yolk and whisk until the mixture is smooth and thick. Add the flour-and-baking soda mixture and stir until incorporated. Add the chocolate chips and stir until evenly distributed. Form the mixture into 16 balls and place on parchment-lined baking sheets, leaving about 2 inches between each ball.

4. Working with one baking sheet at a time, place it in the oven and bake until golden brown, 12 to 16 minutes, rotating the sheet halfway through the bake time. Remove from the oven and let cool to room temperature before serving.

Chocolate, Peanut Butter & Raspberry Curls

Yield: 12 Cookies ◊ Active Time: 20 Minutes ◊ Total Time: 1 Hour

4¼ oz. all-purpose flour

1½ oz. unsweetened cocoa powder

½ teaspoon baking soda

⅛ teaspoon fine sea salt

½ cup unsalted butter, softened and chopped

¾ cup smooth peanut butter, at room temperature

7 oz. sugar

3¾ oz. light brown sugar

1 egg, at room temperature and beaten

1 teaspoon pure vanilla extract

¼ cup raspberry jam

1 Line two baking sheets with parchment paper. Sift the flour, cocoa powder, baking soda, and salt into a mixing bowl and set it aside.

2 Place the butter, peanut butter, sugar, and brown sugar in the work bowl of a stand mixer fitted with the paddle attachment and beat until the mixture is pale and fluffy, scraping down the work bowl as needed. Add the egg and vanilla and beat to incorporate. With the mixer running at low speed, gradually add the dry mixture to the wet mixture and beat until the resulting mixture comes together as a smooth dough.

3 Transfer the dough to a piping bag fit with a star tip. Pipe 2-inch-wide roses onto parchment-lined baking sheets, making sure to leave ½ inch between each cookie. Place the baking sheets in the refrigerator for 1 hour.

4 Preheat the oven to 375°F. Use the butt end of a thin-handled wooden spoon to make a hole in the center of each rose. Spoon 1 teaspoon of jam into each hole.

5 Place the cookies in the oven and bake until they are set, 11 to 14 minutes. Remove the cookies from the oven and let them cool on the baking sheets for a few minutes before transferring them to a wire rack to cool completely.

Chocolate Crinkle Cookies

Yield: 20 Cookies ⋄ Active Time: 45 Minutes ⋄ Total Time: 2 Hours and 30 Minutes

9 oz. dark chocolate (55 to 65 percent)

4½ oz. unsalted butter, softened

7 oz. dark brown sugar

¾ teaspoon pure vanilla extract

2 eggs

7 oz. all-purpose flour

2½ oz. cocoa powder

2 teaspoons baking powder

1 teaspoon kosher salt

2 cups confectioners' sugar, for coating

1. Line two baking sheets with parchment paper. Bring water to a simmer in a small saucepan over low heat. Place the chocolate in a heatproof bowl and place the bowl over the simmering water. Occasionally stir the chocolate until it is melted. Remove the bowl from heat and set it aside.

2. In the work bowl of a stand mixer fitted with the paddle attachment, cream the butter, dark brown sugar, and vanilla on medium speed until the mixture is very light and fluffy, about 5 minutes. Scrape down the work bowl and then beat the mixture for another 5 minutes.

3. Reduce the speed to low, add the melted chocolate, and beat until incorporated, scraping down the work bowl as needed.

4. Add the eggs one at a time and beat until incorporated, again scraping the work bowl as needed. When both eggs have been incorporated, beat for another minute.

5. Add the flour, cocoa powder, baking powder, and salt and beat until the mixture comes together as a smooth dough.

6. Drop 2 oz. portions of the dough on the baking sheets, making sure to leave enough space between them. Place the baking sheets in the refrigerator and let the dough firm up for 1 hour.

7. Preheat the oven to 350°F. Place the confectioners' sugar in a mixing bowl, toss the cookie dough balls in the sugar until completely coated, and then place them back on the baking sheets.

8. Place the cookies in the oven and bake until a cake tester comes out clean after being inserted, 12 to 14 minutes.

9. Remove the cookies from the oven, transfer them to a cooling rack, and let them cool for 20 to 30 minutes before enjoying.

Red Velvet Crinkle Cookies

Yield: 24 Cookies ♦ Active Time: 45 Minutes ♦ Total Time: 2 Hours and 30 Minutes

9 oz. all-purpose flour

2 tablespoons cocoa powder

1½ teaspoons baking powder

½ teaspoon kosher salt

4 oz. unsalted butter, softened

4 oz. sugar

5 oz. light brown sugar

2 eggs

2 teaspoons pure vanilla extract

2 drops of red gel food coloring

2 cups confectioners' sugar, for coating

1. Line two baking sheets with parchment paper. In a mixing bowl, whisk the flour, cocoa powder, baking powder, and salt together. Set the mixture aside.

2. In the work bowl of a stand mixer fitted with the paddle attachment, cream the butter, sugar, and brown sugar on medium speed until the mixture is very light and fluffy, about 5 minutes. Scrape down the work bowl and then beat the mixture for another 5 minutes.

3. Add the eggs one at a time and beat until incorporated, again scraping the work bowl as needed. When both eggs have been incorporated, scrape down the work bowl, add the vanilla and food coloring, and beat for another minute. Add the dry mixture and beat until the resulting mixture comes together as a smooth dough.

4. Drop 2 oz. portions of the dough on the baking sheets, making sure to leave enough space between them. Place the baking sheets in the refrigerator and let the dough firm up for 1 hour.

5. Preheat the oven to 350°F. Place the confectioners' sugar in a mixing bowl, toss the cookie dough balls in the sugar until completely coated, and then place them back on the baking sheets.

6. Place the cookies in the oven and bake until a cake tester comes out clean after being inserted, 12 to 14 minutes.

7. Remove the cookies from the oven, transfer them to a cooling rack, and let them cool for 20 to 30 minutes before enjoying.

Amaretti Cookies

Yield: 50 Cookies ◆ Active Time: 40 Minutes ◆ Total Time: 24 Hours

1¼ cups blanched almonds

5.3 oz. confectioners' sugar

2 tablespoons chopped bitter almonds

2 oz. egg whites

1 teaspoon baker's ammonia

1. Preheat the oven to 390°F. Place the blanched almonds on a baking sheet, place them in the oven, and toast until golden brown, about 5 minutes. Remove the toasted almonds from the oven and let them cool.

2. Place the toasted almonds in a food processor, add the confectioners' sugar and bitter almonds, and pulse until the mixture is finely ground, taking care not to overwork the mixture and release the fat in the almonds.

3. Transfer the mixture to a bowl, add the egg whites and baker's ammonia, and work the resulting mixture until well combined.

4. Cover the bowl with plastic wrap and chill it in the refrigerator overnight.

5. Preheat the oven to 300°F and line two baking sheets with parchment paper. Working with slightly wet hands, form the mixture into balls the size of a small walnut and place them on the baking sheets.

6. Place the amaretti on the baking sheets. Bake the amaretti until they are golden brown, about 20 minutes. Remove the amaretti from the oven, transfer them to wire racks, and let them cool completely before enjoying.

Snowballs

Yield: 36 Cookies ◆ Active Time: 20 Minutes ◆ Total Time: 1 Hour

1½ oz. cream cheese, softened

Zest and juice of 1 lime

6 oz. confectioners' sugar

12½ oz. all-purpose flour

6 oz. caster (superfine) sugar

¼ teaspoon fine sea salt

8 oz. unsalted butter, divided into tablespoons and softened

2 teaspoons pure vanilla extract

1½ cups sweetened shredded coconut, finely chopped

1. Preheat the oven to 350°F and line two baking sheets with parchment paper. Place 1 tablespoon of the cream cheese and the lime juice in a mixing bowl and stir until the mixture is smooth. Add the confectioners' sugar and whisk until the mixture is smooth and thin, adding lime juice as needed until the glaze reaches the desired consistency. Set the glaze aside.

2. Place the flour, caster sugar, salt, and lime zest in a separate mixing bowl and whisk to combine. Add the butter one piece at a time and use a pastry blender to work the mixture until it is a coarse meal. Add the vanilla and remaining cream cheese and work the mixture until it is a smooth dough.

3. Form the mixture into balls and place them on the baking sheets. Place in the oven and bake until the cookies are a light brown, about 15 minutes.

4. Remove the cookies from the oven and let them cool to room temperature. Brush the glaze over the cookies and roll them in the coconut on top. Let the glaze set before serving.

Gingerbread Madeleines

Yield: 16 Madeleines ◆ Active Time: 25 Minutes ◆ Total Time: 3 Hours

2½ oz. unsalted butter, plus more as needed

3½ oz. brown sugar

2 eggs

1-inch piece of fresh ginger, peeled and grated

1¼ teaspoons pure vanilla extract

1½ tablespoons molasses

⅓ cup whole milk

2½ oz. all-purpose flour

2 oz. cake flour

¼ teaspoon baking powder

1½ teaspoons fine sea salt

¼ teaspoon ground cloves

¼ teaspoon freshly grated nutmeg

1 teaspoon cinnamon

1. Place the butter in a small saucepan and cook over medium heat until lightly brown. Remove from heat and let cool to room temperature.

2. Place the butter and brown sugar in the work bowl of a stand mixer fitted with the whisk attachment. Beat on high until light and frothy. Reduce the speed to low, add the eggs one at a time, and beat until incorporated. Add the ginger, vanilla, molasses, and milk and beat until incorporated.

3. Sift the flours and baking powder into a bowl. Add the salt, cloves, nutmeg, and cinnamon and stir to combine.

4. Gradually add the dry mixture to the wet mixture and beat until the dry mixture has been thoroughly incorporated. Transfer the dough to the refrigerator and chill for 2 hours.

5. Preheat the oven to 375°F and brush each shell-shaped depression in the madeleine pan with butter. Place the pan in the freezer for at least 10 minutes.

6. Remove the pan from the freezer and the batter from the refrigerator. Fill each "shell" two-thirds of the way with batter, place the pan in the oven, and bake until a toothpick inserted into the center of a cookie comes out clean, about 12 minutes. Remove from the oven and place the cookies on a wire rack to cool slightly. Serve warm or at room temperature.

Roccocò

Yield: 20 Cookies ◆ Active Time: 1 Hour ◆ Total Time: 1 Hour and 30 Minutes

17.6 oz. unpeeled almonds

17.6 oz. all-purpose flour, plus more as needed

1 teaspoon unsweetened cocoa powder

1½ teaspoons Pisto (see page 266)

1 teaspoon baker's ammonia

17.6 oz. sugar

Zest of 1 orange

Zest of 1 clementine

Zest of ½ lemon

⅓ cup candied orange peels, minced

Pinch of fine sea salt

3½ tablespoons fresh orange juice

½ cup water

1 egg

1 egg yolk

Confectioners' sugar, for dusting

1. Preheat the oven to 350°F. Place the almonds on a baking sheet, place them in the oven, and toast them for 5 minutes. Remove the almonds from the oven and let them cool completely. Leave the oven on.

2. Place the flour, cocoa powder, Pisto, baker's ammonia, sugar, citrus zests, candied orange peels, and salt in the work bowl of a stand mixer fitted with the dough hook.

3. Place the orange juice and water in a measuring cup and warm the mixture to 105°F. With the mixer running on low, gradually add the mixture to the flour mixture until it has all been incorporated and the resulting mixture comes together as a dough.

4. Add the almonds and work the dough until they are incorporated. The dough should be dense and not sticky.

5. Work the dough on low until it is smooth, about 5 minutes.

6. Divide the dough into 3 pieces, place them on a flour-dusted work surface, and roll each piece into a log. Tear the logs into pieces that are approximately 3 oz. and roll them into thin logs.

7. Line two baking sheets with parchment paper. Form each log into a ring and place them on the baking sheets.

8. Place the egg and egg yolk in a bowl and whisk until combined. Brush the rings, inside and out, with the mixture.

9. Place the baking sheets in the oven and bake the roccocò until they are golden brown and hard, about 25 minutes.

10. Remove the roccocò from the oven and let them cool on the baking sheets for a few minutes before transferring them to wire racks to cool completely. Dust the roccocò with confectioners' sugar before serving.

Chocolate-Dipped Orange Cookies

Yield: 24 Cookies ◆ Active Time: 30 Minutes ◆ Total Time: 1 Hour and 45 Minutes

2 tablespoons orange juice

¼ teaspoon ground saffron

4 oz. unsalted butter, softened

9.7 oz. sugar

Pinch of ground cardamom

Pinch of fine sea salt

1 tablespoon light brown sugar

Zest of 1 orange

2 egg yolks

9.9 oz. all-purpose flour

¾ oz. almond flour

¼ teaspoon baking soda

1½ cups dark chocolate chips

1. Preheat the oven to 350°F and line two baking sheets with parchment paper. Place the orange juice in a small saucepan and warm it over medium heat. Remove the pan from heat, add the saffron, and stir until it has dissolved. Set the saffron-infused orange juice aside.

2. Place the butter, sugar, cardamom, salt, brown sugar, and orange zest in the work bowl of a stand mixer fitted with the paddle attachment and beat until it is pale and fluffy. Add the egg yolks and beat until incorporated.

3. Sift the flour, almond flour, and baking soda into a separate mixing bowl and whisk to combine. Gradually add the flour mixture to the butter mixture and beat until the resulting mixture comes together as a dough. Gradually add the saffron-infused orange juice and beat until the dough is smooth.

4. Place the dough in a piping bag fitted with a fluted tip. Pipe 2½-inch-long cookies onto the baking sheets and place them in the oven.

5. Bake the cookies until they are golden brown, 10 to 12 minutes. Remove them from the oven and transfer to wire racks to cool.

6. Place the chocolate chips in a microwave-safe bowl and microwave on medium until they are melted and smooth, removing to stir every 15 seconds. Dip the one end of the cookies into the melted chocolate and let the chocolate set before serving.

8 oz. unsalted butter, softened

7 oz. light brown sugar

1 egg

12 oz. all-purpose flour, plus more as needed

1 teaspoon baking powder

½ teaspoon kosher salt

1½ cups chocolate chips

½ cup walnuts, chopped

Chocolate-Dipped Sugar Cookies

Yield: 48 Cookies ⋄ Active Time: 40 Minutes ⋄ Total Time: 3 Hours

1. In the work bowl of a stand mixer fitted with the paddle attachment, cream the butter and brown sugar on medium speed until the mixture is very light and fluffy, about 5 minutes. Scrape down the work bowl and then beat the mixture for another 5 minutes.
2. Reduce the speed to low, add the egg, and beat until incorporated. Scrape down the work bowl and beat the mixture for 1 minute on medium.
3. Add the flour, baking powder, and salt, reduce the speed to low, and beat until the mixture comes together as a dough. Form the dough into a ball and then flatten it into a disk. Envelop the dough in plastic wrap and refrigerate for 2 hours.
4. Preheat the oven to 350°F and line two baking sheets with parchment paper.
5. Remove the dough from the refrigerator and let it sit on the counter for 5 minutes.
6. Place the dough on a flour-dusted work surface and roll it out until it is approximately ¼ inch thick. Use cookie cutters to cut the dough into the desired shapes and place them on the baking sheets. Form any scraps into a ball, roll it out, and cut into cookies. If the dough becomes too sticky or warm, place it back in the refrigerator for 15 minutes to firm up.
7. Place the cookies in the oven and bake until their edges are lightly golden brown, 8 to 10 minutes. Remove the cookies from the oven, transfer them to a wire rack, and let them cool.
8. Place the chocolate chips in a microwave-safe bowl and microwave on medium until they are melted and smooth, removing to stir every 15 seconds. Dip the one end of the cookies into the melted chocolate and sprinkle some walnuts over the chocolate. Let the chocolate set before serving.

Pizzelles

Yield: 30 to 50 Cookies ✧ Active Time: 40 Minutes ✧ Total Time: 40 Minutes

7.3 oz. all-purpose flour, plus more as needed

2 teaspoons baking powder

½ teaspoon fine sea salt

3 eggs

5¼ oz. sugar

4 oz. unsalted butter, melted

1 teaspoon pure vanilla extract

½ teaspoon anise extract

1. Preheat a pizzelle maker. Combine the flour, baking powder and salt in a small bowl. In the work bowl of a stand mixer fitted with the paddle attachment, beat the eggs and sugar until the mixture is fluffy, 3 to 5 minutes. Slowly add the melted butter, vanilla, and anise and beat until incorporated.

2. Gradually add the dry mixture and beat until the resulting mixture comes together as a smooth batter.

3. Using two spoons, carefully drop the batter onto the center of a well-heated pizzelle maker (teaspoons for 3-inch pizzelles, and tablespoons for 5-inch).

4. Cook until the pizzelles are just lightly brown, about 30 seconds. Gently remove the cookies from the pizzelle maker and transfer them to a wire rack to cool completely.

Peppermint Bars

Yield: 12 Bars ◇ Active Time: 1 Hour ◇ Total Time: 3 Hours and 30 Minutes

For the Crust

8 oz. dark chocolate (55 to 65 percent)

4 oz. unsalted butter

6 oz. sugar

2 oz. light brown sugar

2 tablespoons cocoa powder

¼ teaspoon kosher salt

3 eggs

¾ teaspoon pure vanilla extract

For the Topping

28½ oz. confectioners' sugar

6 tablespoons unsalted butter, softened

½ cup heavy cream

2 cups peppermint candy pieces, plus more for garnish

2 cups Chocolate Ganache (see page 266), warm

1. Preheat the oven to 350°F. Line a 13 x 9-inch baking pan with parchment paper and coat it with nonstick cooking spray. To begin preparations for the crust, fill a small saucepan halfway with water and bring it to a simmer. Place the chocolate and butter in a heatproof bowl, place it over the simmering water, and stir until they are melted and combined. Remove from heat and set aside.

2. In a mixing bowl, whisk the sugar, brown sugar, cocoa powder, and salt together, making sure to break up any clumps. Add the eggs and vanilla, whisk to incorporate, and then add the melted chocolate mixture. Whisk to incorporate, pour the batter into the baking pan, and even the surface with a rubber spatula. Lightly tap the baking pan on the counter to settle the batter and remove any air bubbles.

3. Place in the oven and bake until a cake tester comes out clean, 20 to 30 minutes. Remove from the oven and transfer the pan to a cooling rack.

4. To prepare the topping, place the confectioners' sugar, butter, and heavy cream in the work bowl of a stand mixer fitted with the paddle attachment and cream on low until the mixture comes together. Raise the speed to medium and beat until light and fluffy. Add the peppermint candies and beat until just incorporated.

5. Spread the mixture over the baked crust, using an offset spatula to even it out. Transfer the pan to the refrigerator and chill until the topping is set, about 2 hours.

6. Run a sharp knife along the edge of the pan and carefully remove the bars. Place them on a cutting board and cut them into squares. Drizzle the ganache over the bars, sprinkle the additional peppermint candies on top, and store the bars in the refrigerator until ready to serve.

Peanut Butter Blossoms

Yield: 48 Cookies ◆ Active Time: 15 Minutes ◆ Total Time: 1 Hour

48 milk chocolate kisses

7.3 oz. all-purpose flour

1 teaspoon baking soda

½ teaspoon fine sea salt

4 oz. unsalted butter, softened

½ cup smooth peanut butter

½ cup sugar, plus more to taste

½ cup firmly packed brown sugar

1 egg

1 teaspoon pure vanilla extract

1 Preheat oven to 375°F. Remove the foil wrap from the chocolate kisses. Sift the flour, baking soda, and salt into a mixing bowl. Set the mixture aside.

2 In the work bowl of a stand mixer fitted with the paddle attachment, beat the butter and peanut butter until the mixture is fluffy, about 5 minutes. Add the sugars, egg, and vanilla and beat until incorporated. Gradually add the dry mixture and beat until the resulting mixture comes together as a smooth dough.

3 Form teaspoons of the dough into 1-inch balls, roll them in a bowl of sugar until completely coated, and place them on ungreased baking sheets, making sure to leave enough space between them. Place the cookies in the oven and bake until they are lightly browned, 8 to 10 minutes.

4 Remove the cookies from the oven, top each one with a chocolate kiss, and press down gently. The cookie will crack around the edges, which is precisely what you want.

5 Transfer the cookies to a wire rack and let the cookies cool completely.

Cranberry, Pumpkin Seed & Chocolate Chip Cookies

Yield: 48 Cookies ⋄ Active Time: 15 Minutes ⋄ Total Time: 3 Hours

13¼ oz. all-purpose flour

1 teaspoon baking soda

1 teaspoon fine sea salt

8 oz. unsalted butter, softened

7 oz. light brown sugar

3½ oz. sugar

2 large eggs, at room temperature

2 teaspoons pure vanilla extract

1½ cups chocolate chips

1 cup chopped cranberries

½ cup pumpkin seeds

1. Place the flour, baking soda, and salt in a large mixing bowl and whisk to combine. Set the mixture aside.

2. Place the butter, brown sugar, and sugar in the work bowl of a stand mixer fitted with the paddle attachment and beat until the mixture pale and fluffy, scraping down the work bowl as needed. Reduce the speed to low and incorporate the eggs one at a time. Add the vanilla and beat to incorporate.

3. With the mixer running on low speed, gradually add the dry mixture to the wet mixture and beat until the resulting mixture comes together as a smooth dough. Add the chocolate chips, cranberries, and pumpkin seeds and fold until they are evenly distributed. Cover the dough with plastic wrap and chill it in the refrigerator for 2 hours.

4. Preheat the oven to 350°F and line two baking sheets with parchment paper. Drop tablespoons of the dough onto the baking sheets and, working with one baking sheet at a time, place the cookies in the oven and bake for about 10 minutes, until lightly browned.

5. Remove the cookies from the oven and let them cool on the baking sheets for 5 minutes before transferring them to wire racks to cool completely.

Vegan Ginger Molasses Cookies

Yield: 30 Cookies ◆ Active Time: 20 Minutes ◆ Total Time: 1 Hour and 30 Minutes

3.2 oz. margarine

7.7 oz. sugar, plus more as needed

6.7 oz. brown sugar

3 oz. aquafaba

2½ oz. molasses

11.6 oz. all-purpose flour

2 teaspoons baking soda

½ teaspoon fine sea salt

1 teaspoon ground ginger

1 teaspoon cinnamon

1. Preheat the oven to 325°F. Line two baking sheets with parchment paper.

2. Place the margarine, sugar, and brown sugar in the work bowl of a stand mixer fitted with the paddle attachment and beat until the mixture is light and fluffy. Add the aquafaba and molasses and beat until incorporated.

3. Place the remaining ingredients in a mixing bowl and whisk to combine. With the mixer running on low, gradually add the dry mixture to the wet mixture and beat until the resulting mixture comes together as a smooth dough.

4. Place some sugar in a shallow bowl. Form the dough into 1 oz. balls and roll them in the sugar. Place the cookies on the baking sheets, making sure to leave plenty of space between them. Chill the cookies in the refrigerator for 15 minutes.

5. Place the cookies in the oven and bake until they start to crack and the edges are set, 12 to 15 minutes, rotating the baking sheets halfway through.

6. Remove the cookies from the oven and let them cool on the baking sheets for a few minutes. Transfer the cookies to wire racks and let them cool completely.

Pumpkin Cheesecake Bars

Yield: 20 to 24 Bars ◆ Active Time: 45 Minutes ◆ Total Time: 24 Hours

For the Crust

2 cups finely crushed graham crackers

¼ cup sugar

½ cup unsalted butter

For the Filling

1½ lbs. cream cheese, softened

1 cup sugar

¾ cup light brown sugar

6 large eggs

1 tablespoon pure vanilla extract

1½ teaspoons pumpkin pie spice

1 (14 oz.) can of pumpkin puree

Whipped Cream (see page 267), for topping

Cinnamon, for dusting

1 Preheat the oven to 325°F. Line a 13 x 9-inch baking pan with parchment paper and coat it with nonstick cooking spray. To prepare the crust, place all of the ingredients in a mixing bowl and work the mixture with your hands until combined, soft, and crumbly.

2 Firmly press the crust into the pan, making sure it is flat and even. Place in the oven and bake until the crust begins to brown at the edges, about 20 minutes. Remove the crust from the oven and place the pan on a wire rack. Let the crust cool completely and leave the oven on.

3 To prepare the filling, place the cream cheese, sugar, and brown sugar in a mixing bowl and stir to combine. Add the eggs and vanilla and stir to incorporate. Add the pumpkin pie spice and pumpkin puree and stir until thoroughly combined.

4 Spread the filling over the crust and place the pan in the oven. Bake until the edges of the filling appear set and the center jiggles slightly when you shake the pan.

5 Remove the cheesecake bars from the oven and let them cool completely. Chill the bars in the refrigerator overnight.

6 Remove the bars from the refrigerator, use the parchment paper to lift them out of the pan, and cut them into squares. Top each bar with some Whipped Cream and cinnamon and serve.

Classic Sugar Cookies

Yield: 48 Cookies ◆ Active Time: 40 Minutes ◆ Total Time: 3 Hours

8 oz. unsalted butter, softened

7 oz. light brown sugar

1 egg

12 oz. all-purpose flour, plus more as needed

1 teaspoon baking powder

½ teaspoon kosher salt

1. In the work bowl of a stand mixer fitted with the paddle attachment, cream the butter and brown sugar on medium speed until the mixture is very light and fluffy, about 5 minutes. Scrape down the work bowl and then beat the mixture for another 5 minutes.

2. Reduce the speed to low, add the egg, and beat until incorporated. Scrape down the work bowl and beat the mixture for 1 minute on medium.

3. Add the remaining ingredients, reduce the speed to low, and beat until the mixture comes together as a dough. Form the dough into a ball and then flatten it into a disk. Envelop the dough in plastic wrap and refrigerate for 2 hours.

4. Preheat the oven to 350°F and line two baking sheets with parchment paper.

5. Remove the dough from the refrigerator and let it sit on the counter for 5 minutes.

6. Place the dough on a flour-dusted work surface and roll it out until it is approximately ¼ inch thick. Use cookie cutters to cut the dough into the desired shapes and place them on the baking sheets. Form any scraps into a ball, roll it out, and cut into cookies. If the dough becomes too sticky or warm, place it back in the refrigerator for 15 minutes to firm up.

7. Place the cookies in the oven and bake until lightly golden brown at their edges, 8 to 10 minutes. Remove from the oven, transfer to a wire rack, and let cool for 10 minutes before enjoying or decorating.

Ricciarelli

Yield: 25 Cookies ❖ Active Time: 40 Minutes ❖ Total Time: 25 Hours

2 egg whites

1 teaspoon fresh lemon juice

Seeds of 1 vanilla bean

2 drops of bitter almond extract

Zest of 1 orange

7 oz. almond flour

7 oz. confectioners' sugar, plus more as needed

1. Place the egg whites, lemon juice, vanilla seeds, bitter almond extract, and orange zest in a mixing bowl and whisk until the mixture is foamy.

2. Add the almond flour and confectioners' sugar and whisk until the mixture comes together as a soft dough.

3. Form the dough into a ball, cover it in plastic wrap, and chill it in the refrigerator for 24 hours.

4. Preheat the oven to 300°F and line a baking sheet with parchment paper. Generously dust a work surface with confectioners' sugar and place more on a plate. Place the dough on the work surface and shape it into a 1-inch-thick cylinder. Slice it into 1 oz. pieces, roll them in the confectioners' sugar until coated all over, and form them into ovals or diamonds, flattening and lengthening them.

5. Place the ricciarelli on the baking sheet. Wet your fingers, moisten the cookies, and generously sprinkle more confectioners' sugar over the cookies.

6. Place the cookies in the oven and bake for 5 minutes. Raise the oven's temperature to 350°F and bake until the cookies start to crack, about 5 minutes.

7. Reduce the oven's temperature to 320°F and bake for another 5 minutes. Remove the ricciarelli from the oven, transfer them to a wire rack, and let them cool completely before serving.

Opera Torte, see page 138

Cakes

No confection announces that it is time to celebrate quite like the cake, as the sight of one on the table immediately forces everyone to recognize that something grand is underway.

As such, there is no better time to bake a cake than Christmastime. Not just because a beautiful cake is yet another eye-catching ornament around the house. Not only because its decadent promise creates as much anticipation as what's going to be under the tree on Christmas morning. It's also because in preparing a cake we allow ourselves to take a step back and take the time to construct something impressive and guaranteed to please, reminding ourselves that the holidays are mostly about the smiles we create.

Eggnog Cupcakes

Yield: 24 Cupcakes ◆ **Active Time: 30 Minutes** ◆ **Total Time: 1 Hour and 30 Minutes**

For the Cupcakes

11.4 oz. all-purpose flour

9½ oz. sugar

1¾ teaspoons baking powder

½ teaspoon kosher salt

8 oz. unsalted butter, softened

4 egg whites

½ teaspoon pure vanilla extract

2¾ teaspoons freshly grated nutmeg

1 cup heavy cream

⅓ cup milk

For the Frosting

American Buttercream (see page 265)

1 tablespoon freshly grated nutmeg, plus more for topping

1. Preheat the oven to 350°F. Line a 24-well cupcake pan with paper liners.

2. To begin preparations for the cupcakes, whisk together the flour, sugar, baking powder, and salt in a medium bowl. Set the mixture aside.

3. In the work bowl of a stand mixer fitted with the paddle attachment, combine the butter, egg whites, vanilla, and nutmeg on medium speed. The batter will look separated and broken. Reduce the speed to low, add the dry mixture, and beat until incorporated, scraping the sides of the bowl with a rubber spatula as needed.

4. Gradually add the heavy cream and milk until the mixture comes together as a smooth cake batter. Pour approximately ¼ cup of the batter into each cupcake liner.

5. Place in the oven and bake until the cupcakes are lightly golden brown and baked through, 16 to 20 minutes. Insert a cake tester in the center of each cupcake to check for doneness.

6. Remove from the oven and place the cupcakes on a cooling rack.

7. To prepare the frosting, place the buttercream in the work bowl of a stand mixer fitted with the paddle attachment and add the nutmeg. Beat on medium speed until combined. Spoon the frosting into a piping bag fitted with a plain piping tip, frost the cupcakes, and top each one with a little more nutmeg.

- 7½ oz. all-purpose flour
- 1.8 oz. cocoa powder, plus more as needed
- ¾ lb. sugar
- 1½ teaspoons kosher salt
- ¾ teaspoon baking powder
- 5 oz. canola oil
- 5 eggs
- 5 oz. water
- 7 egg whites
- ½ teaspoon cream of tartar
- Butterfluff Filling (see page 264)
- Chocolate Ganache (see page 266), warm
- Peppermint candies, crushed, for topping (optional)
- White chocolate truffles, for topping (optional)

Chocolate Yule Log

Yield: 10 to 12 Servings ◆ Active Time: 45 Minutes ◆ Total Time: 3 Hours

1. Preheat the oven to 350°F. Line an 18 x 13-inch baking sheet with parchment paper and coat it with nonstick cooking spray.

2. Sift the flour, cocoa powder, 7 oz. of the sugar, the salt, and baking powder into a small bowl. Set the mixture aside.

3. In a medium bowl, whisk the canola oil, eggs, and water until combined. Add the dry mixture and whisk until combined.

4. In the work bowl of a stand mixer fitted with the whisk attachment, whip the egg whites and cream of tartar on high until soft peaks begin to form. Reduce the speed to low and add the remaining sugar a few tablespoons at a time. When all of the sugar has been incorporated, raise the speed back to high and whip until the mixture holds stiff peaks.

5. Remove the work bowl from the mixer. Gently fold half of the meringue into the cake batter. Add the remaining meringue and fold until no white streaks remain. Spread the cake batter over the baking sheet, place it in the oven, and bake until the center of the cake springs back when poked with a finger and a cake tester comes out clean, 10 to 12 minutes. Remove the cake from the oven and immediately dust the top with cocoa powder. Turn the sponge cake onto a fresh piece of parchment paper. Peel the parchment away from the bottom side of the cake. Place a fresh piece of parchment on the bottom of the cake and turn it over so that the dusted side of the cake is facing up.

6. Using a rolling pin, gently roll up the cake into a tight roll, starting with the narrow end. Let the cake cool to room temperature while coiled around the rolling pin.

7. Gently unroll the cake and spread the filling evenly over the top, leaving an approximately ½-inch border around the edges. Carefully roll the cake back up with your hands (do not use the rolling pin). Place the cake roll on a cooling rack that has parchment paper beneath it.

8. Pour the ganache over the cake roll and top with the peppermint candies and white chocolate truffles, if desired. Chill the yule log in the refrigerator for at least 1 hour to let the chocolate set before slicing and serving.

Baumkuchen

Yield: 12 to 16 Servings ◆ Active Time: 30 Minutes ◆ Total Time: 2 Hours

All-purpose flour, as needed

7 oz. unsalted butter, softened

5½ oz. marzipan

2½ oz. confectioners' sugar, sifted

3½ oz. cornstarch

1½ teaspoons pure vanilla extract

Pinch of fine sea salt

2 egg yolks

2 egg whites

5¼ oz. sugar

3 oz. self-rising flour

9 oz. chocolate, chopped

2½ teaspoons canola oil

1 Preheat the oven to 400°F. Line a square 9-inch cake pan with parchment paper and coat it with nonstick cooking spray. Dust the pan with all-purpose flour and knock out any excess.

2 Place the butter in the work bowl of a stand mixer fitted with the paddle attachment and beat until it is light and fluffy. Gradually add the marzipan and beat to incorporate. Add the confectioners' sugar, cornstarch, vanilla, and salt and beat to incorporate. Incorporate the egg yolks one at a time, scraping down the work bowl as necessary.

3 Place the egg whites in a mixing bowl and use a handheld mixer to beat them until they hold soft peaks. Gradually add the sugar and beat until the meringue holds stiff peaks. Add the meringue to the butter-and-marzipan mixture and fold to combine.

4 Sift the flour over the batter and fold until it is incorporated and the batter is smooth.

5 Spoon a small amount of batter onto the parchment paper in the cake pan. Using a pastry brush, spread the batter into a thin layer that completely covers the parchment paper. Place the pan in the oven and bake until the batter is light brown, 2 to 3 minutes. Remove the pan from the oven, brush a thin layer of batter over the cake, and return the pan to the oven. Bake until this layer is also light brown. Repeat the process until you have used all of the batter and the cake is set.

6 Remove the cake from the oven and let it cool completely.

7 Turn the cake out of the pan and cut it into cubes.

8 Fill a small saucepan halfway with water and bring it to a simmer. Place the chocolate and canola oil in a heatproof mixing bowl and place it over the simmering water. Warm the mixture, stirring occasionally, until the chocolate has melted and the mixture is smooth.

9 Dip the cubes into the melted chocolate until they are completely coated. Let the chocolate set before serving.

Red Velvet Cupcakes

Yield: 24 Cupcakes ◇ Active Time: 1 Hour ◇ Total Time: 2 Hours

12¾ oz. cake flour

1 oz. cocoa powder

½ teaspoon kosher salt

1 teaspoon baking soda

13.4 oz. unsalted butter, softened

14½ oz. sugar

6 eggs

1 teaspoon white vinegar

2½ oz. buttermilk

1 teaspoon pure vanilla extract

2 teaspoons red food coloring

½ cup dark chocolate chips

Royal Icing (see page 264)

1. Preheat the oven to 350°F. Line the wells of a 24-well cupcake pan with paper liners.

2. In a medium bowl, whisk together the cake flour, cocoa powder, salt, and baking soda. Set the mixture aside.

3. In the work bowl of a stand mixer fitted with the paddle attachment, cream the butter and sugar on high speed until the mixture is creamy and fluffy, about 5 minutes. Reduce the speed to low, add the eggs two at a time, and beat until incorporated, scraping down the sides of the bowl with a rubber spatula between additions. Add the vinegar, beat until incorporated, and then add the dry mixture. Beat until thoroughly incorporated, add the buttermilk, vanilla, and food coloring, and beat until they have been combined. Add the chocolate chips and fold until they are evenly distributed.

4. Pour approximately ¼ cup of the batter into each cupcake liner.

5. Place the cupcakes in the oven and bake until they are cooked through and a cake tester inserted into their centers comes out clean, 16 to 20 minutes.

6. Remove the cupcakes from the oven, transfer them to a wire rack, and let them cool completely.

7. Decorate the cupcakes with the icing and let it set before serving.

Gluten-Free Vanilla Cake with Orange Marmalade & Cranberry Jam

Yield: 1 Cake ◊ Active Time: 15 Minutes ◊ Total Time: 1 Hour and 30 Minutes

1. Preheat the oven to 350°F. Liberally coat two round 9-inch cake pans with nonstick cooking spray and then lightly dust them with flour, knocking out the excess.
2. Place the butter and sugar in the work bowl of a stand mixer fitted with the paddle attachment and beat on medium until the mixture is light and fluffy. Add the eggs one at a time, beating until each one is incorporated before adding the next. Scrape down the bowl after incorporating each egg. Add the vanilla and beat to incorporate.
3. Place the flour, xanthan gum, baking soda, and salt in a separate mixing bowl and whisk to combine.
4. Divide the flour mixture and the buttermilk into three portions and alternate adding them to the butter-and-sugar mixture. Incorporate each portion completely before adding the next.
5. Transfer the batter to the prepared pans and bang them on the counter to remove any air bubbles and ensure that the batter is spread evenly. Place the pans in the oven and bake until a toothpick inserted into the centers of the cakes comes out with just a few crumbs attached, about 45 minutes.
6. Remove the cakes from the oven and let them cool in the pans for 30 minutes.
7. Remove the cakes from the pans, place them on a wire rack, and let them cool completely.
8. Trim a thin layer off the top of each cake to create a flat surface.
9. Place one cake on a cake stand, place the cranberry jam on top, and spread it with an offset spatula. Place the marmalade on top and carefully spread it over the cake. Place the second cake on top and spread the buttercream over the entire cake. Chill the cake in the refrigerator for 1 hour before topping with the dried cranberries, slicing, and serving.

8½ oz. gluten-free flour, plus more as needed

6 oz. unsalted butter, softened

9.6 oz. sugar

2 eggs, at room temperature

1 teaspoon pure vanilla extract

1 teaspoon xanthan gum

2 teaspoons baking soda

½ teaspoon fine sea salt

1 cup buttermilk

¼ cup cranberry jam

¼ cup orange marmalade

American Buttercream (see page 265)

Dried cranberries or pomegranate arils, for topping

Chocolate Cupcakes

Yield: 24 Cupcakes ◇ Active Time: 40 Minutes ◇ Total Time: 2 Hours

20 oz. sugar

13 oz. all-purpose flour

4 oz. cocoa powder

1 tablespoon baking soda

1½ teaspoons baking powder

1½ teaspoons kosher salt

1½ cups sour cream

¾ cup canola oil

3 eggs

1½ cups brewed coffee, hot

Classic Chocolate Frosting (see page 267)

1. Preheat the oven to 350°F. Line a 24-well cupcake pan with paper liners.

2. In a medium bowl, whisk together the sugar, flour, cocoa powder, baking soda, baking powder, and salt. Sift the mixture into a separate bowl and set it aside.

3. In the work bowl of a stand mixer fitted with the whisk attachment, whip the sour cream, canola oil, and eggs until well combined.

4. Reduce the speed to low, add the dry mixture, and whip until incorporated, scraping down the work bowl as needed. Gradually add the hot coffee and beat until thoroughly incorporated. Pour about ¼ cup of batter into each cupcake liner.

5. Place the cupcakes in the oven and bake until they are cooked through and a cake tester inserted into the center comes out clean, 18 to 22 minutes.

6. Remove the cupcakes from the oven and place them on a wire rack until completely cool.

7. Decorate the cupcakes with the frosting and serve.

Chocolate Souffles

Yield: 6 Souffles ⬥ Active Time: 30 Minutes ⬥ Total Time: 1 Hour

9 oz. sugar, plus more as needed

20 oz. dark chocolate (55 to 65 percent)

4 oz. unsalted butter

19 oz. water, plus more as needed

2 oz. heavy cream

11 eggs, separated

1½ oz. sour cream

½ teaspoon cream of tartar

1 Preheat the oven to 375°F. Coat the insides of six 8 oz. ramekins with nonstick cooking spray. Place 2 tablespoons of sugar in each ramekin and spread it to evenly coat the insides of the dishes. Knock out any excess sugar and set the ramekins aside.

2 Place the dark chocolate and butter in a large heatproof bowl. Add 2 inches of water to a small saucepan and bring it to a simmer. Place the bowl on top and melt the butter and chocolate together over the double boiler.

3 In a medium saucepan, bring the water and heavy cream to a simmer. Remove the chocolate mixture from the double boiler and whisk it into the water-and-cream mixture. Remove the saucepan from heat.

4 Place the egg yolks and the sour cream in a mixing bowl and whisk until combined. Gradually incorporate the cream-and-chocolate mixture, while whisking constantly. Set the mixture aside.

5 In the work bowl of a stand mixer fitted with the whisk attachment, whip the egg whites and cream of tartar on high until the mixture holds stiff peaks. Reduce the speed to medium and gradually incorporate the 9 oz. of sugar. Once all of the sugar has been incorporated, raise the speed back to high and whip until it is a glossy, stiff meringue.

6 Working in three increments, add the meringue to the chocolate base, folding gently with a rubber spatula.

7 Spoon the souffle base to the rims of the ramekins. Gently tap the bottoms of the ramekins with the palm of your hand to remove any air, but not so hard as to deflate the meringue.

8 Place in the oven and bake until the souffles have risen significantly and set on the outside, but are still jiggly at the center, 25 to 27 minutes. Remove from the oven and serve immediately.

Gluten-Free Almond Torte

Yield: 1 Cake ♦ Active Time: 40 Minutes ♦ Total Time: 2 Hours

2½ oz. gluten-free flour

¼ teaspoon xanthan gum

¾ teaspoon baking powder

¼ teaspoon kosher salt

4 oz. almond paste

4 oz. unsalted butter, softened

4.7 oz. sugar

¼ teaspoon pure vanilla extract

¼ teaspoon almond extract

3 eggs

½ cup slivered almonds

Almond Syrup (see page 268)

Confectioners' sugar, for dusting

1 Preheat the oven to 375°F. Line a round 9-inch cake pan with parchment paper and coat it with nonstick cooking spray.

2 In a medium bowl, whisk together the flour, xanthan gum, baking powder, and salt. Set the mixture aside.

3 In the work bowl of a stand mixer fitted with the paddle attachment, cream the almond paste, butter, sugar, vanilla, and almond extract on high until the mixture is smooth and fluffy, about 10 minutes.

4 Reduce the speed to low and incorporate the eggs one at a time. Scrape down the sides of the bowl with a rubber spatula between each addition. Add the dry mixture, beat until combined, and raise the speed to high. Beat the mixture for 2 minutes to thicken it.

5 Pour the batter into the prepared cake pan. Bang the pan on the countertop to evenly distribute the batter and remove any air bubbles. Sprinkle the slivered almonds over the batter and place it in the oven.

6 Bake the torte until it is lightly golden brown and a cake tester inserted into the center comes out clean, 20 to 25 minutes.

7 Remove from the oven, transfer the torte to a cooling rack, and let it cool completely.

8 Gently brush the syrup over the torte and dust it with confectioners' sugar before slicing and serving.

Orange & Cardamom Cake

Yield: 1 Cake ◆ Active Time: 20 Minutes ◆ Total Time: 2 Hours and 30 Minutes

- 1 lb. all-purpose flour
- 1 teaspoon baking powder
- 1½ teaspoons baking soda
- 2 teaspoons cardamom
- ½ teaspoon cinnamon
- ½ teaspoon kosher salt
- 8 oz. unsalted butter, softened
- 11 oz. sugar
- Zest of 2 oranges
- 4 eggs
- 2 cups sour cream
- Confectioners' sugar, for dusting

1. Preheat the oven to 350°F. Coat a 12-cup Bundt pan with nonstick cooking spray.

2. Place the flour, baking powder, baking soda, cardamom, cinnamon, and salt in a mixing bowl and whisk to combine.

3. In the work bowl of a stand mixer fitted with the paddle attachment, cream the butter, sugar, and orange zest on medium until it is light and fluffy, about 5 minutes.

4. Reduce the speed to low and incorporate the eggs one at a time, scraping down the work bowl as needed. Add the sour cream, raise the speed to medium, and beat to incorporate. Add the dry mixture, reduce the speed to low, and beat until the mixture is a smooth batter.

5. Pour the batter into the pan and tap it on the counter to remove any air bubbles and ensure the batter is spread evenly.

6. Place the cake in the oven and bake until a cake tester inserted into the center comes out clean, 45 to 55 minutes.

7. Remove the cake from the oven and place the pan on a wire rack to cool for 1 hour.

8. Remove the cake from the pan, dust it with confectioners' sugar, and enjoy.

Black Forest Cake

Yield: 1 Cake ⋄ Active Time: 1 Hour ⋄ Total Time: 3 Hours and 30 Minutes

20 oz. sugar

13 oz. all-purpose flour

4 oz. cocoa powder

1 tablespoon baking soda

1½ teaspoons baking powder

1½ teaspoons kosher salt

1½ cups sour cream

¾ cup canola oil

3 eggs

1½ cups brewed coffee, hot

2 batches of Whipped Cream (see page 267)

2 cups cherry jam

Dark chocolate, shaved, for garnish

2 cups Luxardo maraschino cherries, for topping

1. Preheat the oven to 350°F. Line three round 8-inch cake pans with parchment paper and coat them with nonstick cooking spray.

2. In a medium bowl, sift the sugar, flour, cocoa powder, baking soda, baking powder, and salt into a mixing bowl and set it aside.

3. In the work bowl of a stand mixer fitted with the whisk attachment, combine the sour cream, canola oil, and eggs on medium speed. Reduce the speed to low, add the dry mixture, and beat until combined. Scrape the sides of the work bowl with a rubber spatula as needed.

4. With the mixer running on low, gradually add the hot coffee and beat until fully incorporated. Pour 1½ cups of batter into each cake pan. Bang the pans on the counter to distribute the batter evenly and remove any air bubbles.

5. Place the cakes in the oven and bake until browned and cooked through, 25 to 30 minutes. Insert a cake tester in the center of each cake to check for doneness. Remove the cakes from the oven, transfer them to a cooling rack, and let them cool completely.

6. Trim a thin layer off the top of each cake to create a flat surface. Transfer 2 cups of the Whipped Cream into a piping bag and cut a ½-inch slit in the bag.

7. Place one cake on a cake stand and pipe one ring of cream around the edge. Place 1 cup of the cherry jam in the center and level it with an offset spatula. Place the second cake on top and repeat the process with the Whipped Cream and cherry jam. Place the last cake on top and spread 1½ cups of the Whipped Cream over the entire cake using an offset spatula. Refrigerate the cake for at least 1 hour.

8. Garnish the cake with the shaved chocolate and Luxardo cherries before slicing and serving.

Coconut Cake

Yield: 1 Cake ◇ Active Time: 1 Hour ◇ Total Time: 3 Hours

1. Preheat the oven to 350°F. Line three round 8-inch cake pans with parchment paper and coat them with nonstick cooking spray.
2. To begin preparations for the cakes, place the flour, baking powder, and salt in a mixing bowl and whisk to combine. Set the mixture aside.
3. In the work bowl of a stand mixer fitted with the paddle attachment, cream the butter and sugar on medium for 5 minutes.
4. Reduce the speed to low and incorporate the eggs one at a time, scraping down the work bowl as needed.
5. Add the dry mixture, beat until combined, and then add the remaining ingredients. Beat until incorporated.
6. Pour 1½ cups of batter into each cake pan. Bang the pans on the countertop to spread the batter and to remove any possible air bubbles.
7. Place the cakes in the oven and bake until they are lightly golden brown and baked through, 20 to 25 minutes. Insert a cake tester in the center of each cake to check for doneness.
8. Remove from the oven and place the cakes on a cooling rack. Let them cool completely.
9. To begin preparations for the frosting, place the buttercream and coconut extract in a mixing bowl and whisk until combined. Set the frosting aside.
10. Trim a thin layer off the top of each cake to create a flat surface.
11. Place one cake on a cake stand. Place half of the jam on top and spread it over the cake with an offset spatula. Place 1 cup of the buttercream in the center and level it with an offset spatula. Place the second cake on top and repeat the process with the jam and buttercream. Place the last cake on top and spread 1 cup of the buttercream over the entire cake using an offset spatula. Sprinkle the coconut over the top and side of the cake.
12. Refrigerate the cake for at least 1 hour before slicing and serving.

For the Cakes

8 oz. cake flour

2¼ teaspoons baking powder

½ teaspoon kosher salt

6 oz. unsalted butter, softened

11 oz. sugar

3 eggs

1 teaspoon pure vanilla extract

2 teaspoons coconut extract

1 cup coconut milk

½ cup sweetened shredded coconut

For the Frosting

American Buttercream (see page 265)

1 teaspoon coconut extract

1 cup raspberry jam

2 cups sweetened shredded coconut

Chocolate Beet Cake

Yield: 1 Cake ◆ Active Time: 45 Minutes ◆ Total Time: 3 Hours and 15 Minutes

2 medium red beets, rinsed

6 oz. all-purpose flour

1 oz. cocoa powder

1¼ teaspoons baking powder

¼ teaspoon kosher salt

8¾ oz. dark chocolate

8¾ oz. unsalted butter

5 tablespoons milk

6 eggs

8¾ oz. sugar

American Buttercream (see page 265)

1. Coat a tall 9-inch springform pan with nonstick cooking spray.

2. Place the beets in a large saucepan, cover them with water, and bring to a boil. Cook the beets until they are very tender when poked with a knife, about 1 hour. Drain and let the beets cool. When cool enough to handle, place the beets under cold, running water and rub off their skins. Cut the beets into 1-inch chunks, place them in a food processor, and puree. Set the puree aside.

3. Preheat the oven to 350°F. Whisk the flour, cocoa powder, baking powder, and salt together in a small bowl. Set the mixture aside.

4. Bring a small saucepan filled halfway with water to a gentle simmer. Add the dark chocolate and butter to a heatproof mixing bowl and set it over the simmering water until the mixture melts, stirring occasionally. Remove the bowl from heat and set aside.

5. Heat the milk in a clean saucepan, warm it over medium-low heat until it starts to steam, and pour it into the chocolate mixture. Stir to combine, add the eggs and sugar, and whisk until incorporated. Add the beet puree, stir to incorporate, and add the dry mixture. Whisk until the mixture comes together as a smooth batter.

6. Pour the batter into the prepared pan, place it in the oven, and bake until a cake tester comes out clean after being inserted into the center, 40 to 45 minutes. Remove from the oven, transfer the cake to a cooling rack, and let it cool completely.

7. Carefully remove the cake from the pan and transfer it to a cake stand. Spread the buttercream over the cake and chill it in the refrigerator for at least 1 hour before slicing and serving.

Bolo Rei

Yield: 1 Cake ❖ Active Time: 40 Minutes ❖ Total Time: 4 Hours

⅓ cup whole milk

1¾ teaspoons active dry yeast

12¾ oz. all-purpose flour, plus more as needed

1.3 oz. confectioners' sugar

¼ teaspoon freshly grated nutmeg

1 teaspoon lemon zest

2 eggs

1 egg yolk

1 teaspoon orange blossom water

3 oz. unsalted butter, cut into small pieces

1 teaspoon fine sea salt

1 cup candied fruit, roughly chopped, plus more for topping

5 tablespoons warm water (110°F)

3 tablespoons sugar

1. Place the milk in a saucepan and warm it to 100°F. Add the yeast, gently stir, and let the mixture rest until it starts to foam, about 10 minutes.

2. Place the mixture in a large mixing bowl. Add the flour, confectioners' sugar, nutmeg, lemon zest, one of the eggs, the egg yolk, and orange blossom water and beat until combined.

3. Transfer the dough to the work bowl of a stand mixer fitted with the dough hook. Work the dough and gradually incorporate the butter. When all of the butter has been incorporated, add the salt and candied fruit. Work the mixture until it is very smooth. This should take about 20 minutes. Place the dough in a naturally warm spot and let it rise until it has doubled in size, about 1 to 1½ hours.

4. Transfer the dough to flour-dusted work surface and shape it into a ball. Place the ball in a 13 x 9-inch baking pan lined with parchment paper and flatten it slightly. Make a small hole in the center of the dough and use your hands to gradually enlarge the hole, creating a ring. Cover the dough with a kitchen towel and let stand for 1 hour.

5. Preheat the oven to 320°F. Place the remaining egg and 1 tablespoon of the warm water in a measuring cup and beat to combine. Brush the cake with the egg wash. Place it in the oven and bake until the cake is golden brown and a cake tester inserted into the center comes out clean, about 30 minutes.

6. Remove the cake from the oven. Place the sugar and the remaining warm water in a mixing bowl and stir until the sugar has dissolved. Brush the hot cake with the glaze and top with additional candied fruit. Let the cake cool completely before slicing and serving.

Lamingtons

Yield: 12 to 16 Servings ⋄ Active Time: 45 Minutes ⋄ Total Time: 2 Hours

For the Cake

4 eggs, separated

6.1 oz. all-purpose flour

2 ⅔ teaspoons baking powder

Pinch of fine sea salt

4.7 oz. avocado oil

7 oz. sugar

4.7 oz. whole milk

For the Coating

10 oz. dark chocolate

1 cup unsalted butter

1 cup whole milk

4 cups shredded coconut

1 Preheat the oven to 350°F. Line a 13 x 9-inch baking pan with parchment paper. To begin preparations for the cake, place the egg whites in a mixing bowl and beat with a handheld mixer until they hold soft peaks. Set the egg whites aside.

2 Combine the flour, baking powder, and salt in a mixing bowl and stir to combine. Place egg yolks, avocado oil, sugar, and milk in the work bowl of a stand mixer fitted with the paddle attachment and beat until the mixture is fluffy. With the mixer running on low, gradually add the flour mixture and beat until the resulting mixture comes together as a smooth batter. Add the beaten egg whites and fold to incorporate.

3 Pour the batter into the prepared pan and place it in the oven. Bake until a cake tester inserted into the center of the cake comes out clean, 20 to 25 minutes.

4 Remove the cake from the oven and let it cool in the pan for 45 minutes.

5 When the cake is close to done cooling, begin preparations for the coating. Fill a small saucepan halfway with water and bring it to a simmer. Place the chocolate, butter, and milk in a heatproof bowl and place it over the simmering water. Stir until the chocolate has melted and the mixture is smooth. Remove the bowl from heat and set it aside. Place the coconut in a shallow dish.

6 Cut the cake into cubes, dip them into the chocolate sauce until they are completely coated, and then roll them in the coconut.

7 Let the chocolate set before serving the lamingtons.

Chocolate & Orange Financiers

Yield: 20 Financiers ◆ **Active Time: 20 Minutes** ◆ **Total Time: 1 Hour and 30 Minutes**

6.7 oz. confectioners' sugar

3.2 oz. hazelnut flour

2 oz. all-purpose flour

0.9 oz. egg whites

6 oz. unsalted butter, melted, plus more as needed

½ teaspoon orange zest

Chocolate Ganache (see page 266), warm

1 Preheat the oven to 450°F. Sift the sugar, hazelnut flour, and all-purpose flour into a bowl. Add the egg whites and stir until thoroughly combined. Add the melted butter and stir until the mixture comes together as a smooth batter.

2 Coat the financier molds with butter and divide the batter between the molds. Place the molds on baking sheets and place them in the oven. Bake for 7 minutes and reduce the oven's temperature to 400°F.

3 Bake until the financiers are golden brown and a cake tester inserted into them comes out with just a few crumbs attached, 6 to 8 minutes. Turn off the oven and let the financiers rest in the warm oven for 5 minutes.

4 Remove the financiers from the oven and let them cool completely.

5 Remove the financiers from the molds, dip the bottoms into the ganache until they are completely coated, and let the chocolate set before serving.

Brown Butter Cake

Yield: 1 Cake ◊ Active Time: 1 Hour ◊ Total Time: 3 Hours and 30 Minutes

- 1½ lbs. all-purpose flour
- 1 tablespoon baking powder
- 2 teaspoons kosher salt
- 1 lb. Brown Butter (see page 268)
- 1 lb. sugar
- 8 eggs
- American Buttercream (see page 265)
- Caramelized White Chocolate (see page 269), cooled slightly

1. Preheat the oven to 350°F. Line three round 8-inch cake pans with parchment paper and coat them with nonstick cooking spray.

2. Sift the flour, baking powder, and salt into a medium bowl and set the mixture aside.

3. In the work bowl of a stand mixer fitted with the paddle attachment, cream the Brown Butter and sugar on high until the mixture is smooth and creamy, about 5 minutes.

4. Incorporate the eggs two at a time, scraping down the sides of the work bowl with a rubber spatula in between each addition. Reduce the speed to low, add the dry mixture, and beat until combined.

5. Pour 1½ cups of batter into each cake pan. Bang the pans on the countertop to evenly distribute the batter and remove any air bubbles.

6. Place the cakes in the oven and bake until they are lightly golden brown and baked through, 35 to 40 minutes. Insert a cake tester in the center of each cake to check for doneness. Remove from the oven, transfer to a cooling rack, and let the cakes cool completely.

7. Trim a thin layer off the top of each cake to create a flat surface. Place one cake on a cake stand and pipe one ring of buttercream around the edge. Place 1 cup of the buttercream in the center and level it with an offset spatula. Place the second cake on top and repeat the process with the buttercream. Place the last cake on top and spread 1½ cups of the buttercream over the entire cake using an offset spatula.

8. Place the Caramelized White Chocolate in a piping bag fitted with a plain tip and pipe swirls on top of the cake. Place the cake in the refrigerator for 1 hour before slicing and serving.

Spice Cake

Yield: 1 Cake ⋄ Active Time: 1 Hour ⋄ Total Time: 3 Hours and 30 Minutes

14 oz. all-purpose flour

2 teaspoons baking soda

1 tablespoon baking powder

2 teaspoons cinnamon

2 teaspoons ground cloves

2 teaspoons freshly grated nutmeg

1 teaspoon ground ginger

1 teaspoon kosher salt

8 eggs

¾ lb. sugar

3 oz. light brown sugar

¾ lb. pumpkin puree

1 cup canola oil

2 teaspoons pure vanilla extract

4 oz. buttermilk

¾ lb. unsalted butter, melted

Confectioners' sugar, for dusting

1. Preheat the oven to 350°F. Coat a 12-cup Bundt pan with nonstick cooking spray.

2. Sift the flour, baking soda, baking powder, cinnamon, cloves, nutmeg, ginger, and salt into a mixing bowl. Set the mixture aside.

3. In the work bowl of a stand mixer fitted with the whisk attachment, beat the eggs, sugar, brown sugar, pumpkin puree, canola oil, and vanilla on medium until combined. Add the buttermilk and melted butter and beat until incorporated.

4. Reduce the speed to low, add the dry mixture, and beat until the resulting mixture comes together as a smooth batter. Pour the batter into the cake pan and bang it on the counter to evenly distribute the batter and remove any air bubbles.

5. Place the cake in the oven and bake until it is lightly golden brown and a cake tester inserted into the center comes out clean. 45 minutes to 1 hour.

6. Remove the cake from the oven, transfer the cake to a cooling rack, and let it cool completely.

7. Sprinkle confectioners' sugar over the top of the cake and serve.

Opera Torte

Yield: 1 Cake ◆ Active Time: 3 Hours ◆ Total Time: 3 Hours and 45 Minutes

For the Joconde

5 oz. fine almond flour

5 oz. confectioners' sugar

1 oz. all-purpose flour

5 eggs

5 egg whites

¼ teaspoon kosher salt

2 tablespoons sugar

For the Coffee Syrup

½ cup water

½ cup sugar

1 tablespoon ground espresso

For the Hazelnut & Praline Crunch

4 oz. dark chocolate (55 to 65 percent)

4 oz. praline paste

3 oz. feuilletine flakes

For the Mocha Cream

1 cup sugar

¼ cup water

6 egg yolks

3 tablespoons espresso powder

8 oz. unsalted butter, softened

Chocolate Ganache (see page 266), at room temperature

---

1. Preheat the oven to 400°F. Coat two 13 x 9-inch baking pans with nonstick cooking spray.

2. To begin preparations for the joconde, sift the almond flour, confectioners' sugar, and all-purpose flour into a large bowl. Add the eggs and whisk until combined. Set the mixture aside.

3. In the work bowl of a stand mixer, fitted with the whisk attachment, whip the egg whites and salt on high until soft peaks begin to form. Reduce the speed to low and gradually incorporate the sugar. Raise the speed back to high and continue to whip until stiff peaks form. Add the meringue to the dry mixture and fold until thoroughly incorporated.

4. Divide the batter between the two prepared pans, place them in the oven, and bake until they are set and lightly browned, 8 to 10 minutes. Remove from the oven, transfer to a cooling rack, and let them cool completely.

5. To prepare the coffee syrup, place the water, sugar, and espresso in a small saucepan and bring to a simmer over medium heat while stirring frequently to dissolve the sugar and espresso. Remove the pan from heat and let the syrup cool completely.

THE CHRISTMAS BAKING COOKBOOK

6. To prepare the hazelnut and praline crunch, bring a small saucepan filled halfway with water to a gentle simmer. Place the chocolate in a small heatproof bowl, place it over the simmering water, and stir until the chocolate has melted. Remove from heat, stir in the praline paste and the feuilletine flakes, and spread the mixture over the two joconde. Place the cakes in the refrigerator.

7. To begin preparations for the mocha cream, place the sugar and water in a small saucepan over high heat. Cook until the mixture reaches 245°F on a candy thermometer.

8. While the sugar and water are heating up, place the egg yolks and espresso powder in the work bowl of a stand mixer fitted with the whisk attachment and whip the mixture on high.

9. When the syrup reaches the correct temperature, gradually add it to the egg yolk mixture. Continue to whip on high until the mixture cools slightly. Reduce the speed to low and gradually add the softened butter. When all of the butter has been incorporated, raise the speed back to high and whip the mixture until smooth and fluffy. Set the mocha cream aside.

10. Remove both cakes from the refrigerator and carefully remove them from the pans. Place one cake on a serving tray with the coated layer facing down. Brush the cake with some of the coffee syrup and spread half of the mocha cream over the top. Lay the second cake on top so that the mocha and hazelnut layers are touching. Brush the top of this cake with the remaining coffee syrup and then spread the remaining mocha cream over the cake.

11. Place the cake in the refrigerator and chill it for 30 minutes.

12. Spread the Chocolate Ganache over the cake and let it sit for 10 minutes. To serve, use a hot knife to cut the cake into rectangles.

Note: Feuilletine flakes are a crispy confection made from thin, sweetened crepes. They can be found at many baking shops and are also available online.

Flourless Chocolate Torte

Yield: 1 Cake ◆ Active Time: 30 Minutes ◆ Total Time: 3 Hours and 30 Minutes

- 9 oz. dark chocolate (55 to 65 percent)
- 4 oz. unsalted butter
- ¼ cup water, plus more as needed
- Pinch of kosher salt
- 3 oz. sugar
- 3 eggs
- ½ teaspoon pure vanilla extract
- Cocoa powder, for dusting
- Confectioners' sugar, for dusting

1. Preheat the oven to 375°F. Line a round 9-inch cake pan with parchment paper and coat it with nonstick cooking spray.

2. Fill a small saucepan halfway with water and bring it to a gentle simmer. In a heatproof medium bowl, combine the chocolate and butter. Place the bowl over the simmering water and stir the mixture with a rubber spatula until it has melted and is smooth. Remove the mixture from heat and set it aside.

3. In another small saucepan, bring the water, salt, and sugar to a boil over medium heat. Pour the mixture into the melted chocolate and whisk to combine. Incorporate the eggs and vanilla and then pour the batter into the prepared cake pan.

4. Place the torte in the oven and bake until it is set and the internal temperature reaches 200°F, 25 to 30 minutes. Remove the torte from the oven and let it cool on a wire rack for 30 minutes.

5. Place the torte in the refrigerator and chill it for 2 hours.

6. Run a paring knife along the edge of the pan and invert the torte onto a serving plate. Dust the top of the torte with cocoa powder and confectioners' sugar, slice, and serve.

Pannettone, see page 172

Breads
& Breakfast Treats

There can be no debate about what gets people excited as Christmas approaches—gifts and sweet treats.

But as one cannot, sadly, subsist on sweets alone, there are points during the holiday season where baked goods other than the sugary confections everyone loves are called for. A generously buttered scone or piece of toast supplies a reason for people to linger around the breakfast table a little longer. A home feels just a little more comfortable when it is filled with the aroma of freshly baked bread. The recipes in this chapter provide the backbone for your holiday celebrations, ensuring that each and every meal is touched by a delicious baked good.

Classic Gingerbread

Yield: 1 Loaf ◆ Active Time: 15 Minutes ◆ Total Time: 1 Hour And 30 Minutes

- 7.4 oz. all-purpose flour
- ½ teaspoon kosher salt
- ⅛ teaspoon baking soda
- 2½ teaspoons ground ginger
- 1½ teaspoons cinnamon
- 1 teaspoon freshly grated nutmeg
- ½ teaspoon ground cloves
- ½ teaspoon allspice
- ¼ cup molasses
- ¼ cup sour cream
- 8 oz. unsalted butter, softened
- 8 oz. dark brown sugar
- 4 eggs
- Confectioners' sugar, for topping

1. Preheat the oven to 350°F. Coat a square 8-inch baking pan with nonstick cooking spray.

2. Place the flour, salt, baking soda, ginger, cinnamon, nutmeg, cloves, and allspice in a mixing bowl and whisk to combine. Set the mixture aside.

3. Combine the molasses and sour cream in a measuring cup and set the mixture aside.

4. In the work bowl of a stand mixer fitted with the paddle attachment, cream the butter and brown sugar until the mixture is light and fluffy, about 5 minutes. Add half of the dry mixture and beat until incorporated. Add half of the molasses mixture, beat until incorporated, and then add the remaining dry mixture. Beat to incorporate, add the remaining molasses mixture and the eggs, and beat until the resulting mixture comes together as a smooth batter.

5. Pour the batter into the prepared pan, place it in the oven, and bake until a cake tester inserted into the center of the bread comes out clean, 50 to 60 minutes.

6. Remove the pan from the oven and place it on a wire rack. Let the bread cool completely. Sprinkle confectioners' sugar over the gingerbread before slicing and serving.

Harvest Sourdough Bread

Yield: 1 Boule ◇ Active Time: 1 Hour and 30 Minutes ◇ Total Time: 24 Hours

1. Place the water and flours in the work bowl of a stand mixer fitted with the dough hook and work the mixture on low for 6 minutes. Remove the bowl from the mixer and cover it with plastic wrap. Let the dough sit at room temperature for 1 hour to allow the dough to autolyse.

2. Place the work bowl back on the mixer and add the cranberries, seeds, starter, and salt. Knead the mixture at low speed until the dough starts to come together, about 2 minutes. Increase the speed to medium and knead until the dough is elastic and pulls away from the side of the bowl.

3. Shape the dough into a ball and spray the seam side with water.

4. Dust a 9-inch banneton (proofing basket) with bread flour. Place the dough in the proofing basket, seam side down. Cover the bread with plastic wrap and let it sit on the counter for 2 hours.

5. Place the proofing basket in the refrigerator and let the dough rest overnight.

6. Preheat the oven to 450°F and place a baking stone on a rack positioned in the middle.

7. Dust a peel with bread flour and gently turn the bread onto the peel so that the seam is facing up.

8. With a very sharp knife, carefully score the dough just off center, making sure the knife is at a 45-degree angle to the dough.

9. Gently slide the sourdough onto the baking stone. Spray the oven with 5 spritzes of water and bake the bread for 20 minutes.

10. Open the oven, spray the oven with 5 more spritzes, and bake until the crust is golden brown and the internal temperature is at least 210°F, about 20 minutes.

11. Remove the bread from the oven, place it on a wire rack, and let it cool completely before slicing.

1 cup water, at room temperature

14.1 oz. bread flour, plus more as needed

1.3 oz. whole wheat flour

¼ cup dried cranberries

2 tablespoons pumpkin seeds

2 tablespoons sunflower seeds

2 tablespoons poppy seeds

2 tablespoons chia seeds

8 oz. Sourdough Starter (see page 270)

2 teaspoons kosher salt

Stollen

Yield: 2 Stollen ◆ Active Time: 2 Hours ◆ Total Time: 4 Days

- ⅔ cup raisins
- ⅔ cup golden raisins
- ½ cup dried cherries
- ⅓ cup Grand Marnier
- 1 cup slivered almonds
- 2¼ teaspoons active dry yeast
- ½ cup lukewarm milk (90°F)
- 17 oz. all-purpose flour
- 8.3 oz. sugar
- 2¾ teaspoons ground ginger
- 1 teaspoon fine sea salt
- 1 teaspoon cinnamon
- 1 teaspoon cardamom
- 1 teaspoon freshly grated nutmeg
- 1 teaspoon lemon zest
- Seeds of ½ vanilla bean, pod reserved
- 1 lb. unsalted butter, melted
- 2 large egg yolks
- ½ cup chopped candied ginger
- ½ cup candied citrus peels
- 1½ cups confectioners' sugar, plus more for dusting

1. Place the raisins, cherries, and Grand Marnier in a mason jar. Place the almonds and ¼ cup water in another mason jar. Seal and let the mixtures sit at room temperature overnight.

2. Place the yeast and milk in the work bowl of a stand mixer fitted with the paddle attachment and mix on low. Add 1 cup of flour and beat the mixture until it comes together as a soft, sticky dough; this is the levain. Coat a bowl with nonstick cooking spray, place the dough in it, and cover the bowl with plastic wrap. Place the bowl in a naturally warm spot and let the dough rise for 45 minutes.

3. Place the remaining flour, 3 tablespoons of sugar, ½ teaspoon of ground ginger, the salt, cinnamon, cardamom, nutmeg, lemon zest, and vanilla seeds and beat to combine. With the mixer running, add half of the melted butter. Beat on low for 1 minute and then add the egg yolks. Beat until incorporated.

4. With the mixer running on low, add the levain in three increments, beating until each one is thoroughly incorporated. Raise the speed to medium and beat until the dough is smooth and glossy, about 6 minutes.

5. Drain the almonds and add them to the dough along with the candied ginger and candied citrus peels. Beat on low until they are evenly distributed. Add the raisins, cherries, and Grand Marnier and mix on low until incorporated.

6. Place the dough on a flour-dusted work surface and knead it until the fruits, almonds, candied ginger, and candied citrus peels are inside the dough rather than stuck on the surface, and dough is smooth and glossy, about 5 minutes.

7. Coat a bowl with nonstick cooking spray and place the dough in it. Cover it with plastic wrap and let the dough rise in a naturally warm spot for 1 hour.

8. Place the dough on a flour-dusted work surface and knead it. Place it back in the bowl, cover it with plastic wrap, and let it rise for another hour.

9. Divide the dough into two pieces and shape each one into an oval that is about 8 inches long. Stack two rimmed baking sheets on top of each other and line the top pan with parchment paper. Place the dough on the stacked pans and cover them with plastic. Let the stollen rise for 1 hour at room temperature.

10. Preheat the oven to 350°F. Remove the plastic that is covering the stollen and place the stollen in the oven. Bake until they are dark brown and their internal temperature is at least 190°F.

11. Remove the stollen from the oven and transfer the top pan to a wire rack. Brush the hot stollen with the remaining melted butter. Combine the remaining sugar and remaining ground ginger and sprinkle the mixture all over the stollen. Let them cool on the pan.

12. Cover the stollen loosely with aluminum foil and let them rest overnight.

13. Sprinkle the stollen with the confectioners' sugar, making sure they are completely coated. Cover the stollen with plastic wrap and let them sit at room temperature for 2 days.

14. Sprinkle additional confectioners' sugar over the stollen and serve.

Stollen, see page 148

Gingerbread Muffins

Yield: 12 Muffins ◆ Active Time: 25 Minutes ◆ Total Time: 1 Hour and 30 Minutes

4 oz. unsalted butter, chopped

6 oz. dark molasses

11.8 oz. all-purpose flour

1½ teaspoons baking soda

¼ teaspoon salt

1½ teaspoons cinnamon

1¼ teaspoons ground ginger

½ teaspoon ground cloves

3½ oz. dark brown sugar

1 egg, at room temperature

4 oz. crème fraiche, at room temperature

½ cup whole milk, at room temperature

½ cup chopped candied almonds

Confectioners' sugar, for dusting

1. Preheat the oven to 425°F. Coat a 12-well muffin pan with nonstick cooking spray.

2. Place the butter and molasses in a saucepan and gently warm it over low heat until it is melted and smooth. Remove the pan from heat and let the mixture cool.

3. Place the flour, baking soda, salt, cinnamon, ginger, and cloves in a mixing bowl and whisk to combine.

4. Stir the brown sugar, egg, crème fraiche, and milk into the molasses mixture. Add the molasses mixture to the dry mixture and stir until the resulting mixture just comes together as a slightly lumpy batter. Add the candied almonds and fold until evenly distributed.

5. Fill the wells of the muffin pan with the batter and place the pan in the oven. Bake for 8 minutes, lower the oven's temperature to 350°F, and bake until a cake tester inserted into the centers of the muffins comes out clean, about 15 minutes.

6. Remove the muffins from the oven and let them cool in the pan for 10 minutes. Transfer the muffins to a wire rack and let them cool completely. Sprinkle confectioners' sugar over the muffins before serving.

Stout Gingerbread

Yield: 1 Loaf ◆ Active Time: 15 Minutes ◆ Total Time: 1 Hour and 30 Minutes

8½ oz. all-purpose flour

1½ teaspoons baking powder

2 tablespoons ground ginger

½ teaspoon cinnamon

½ teaspoon ground cloves

¼ teaspoon freshly grated nutmeg

¼ teaspoon fine sea salt

1 cup molasses

1 cup stout

1½ teaspoons baking soda

3 eggs

4 oz. sugar

4 oz. dark brown sugar

¾ cup canola oil

Chocolate Ganache (see page 266), warm

Confectioners' sugar, for dusting

1. Preheat the oven to 350°F. Coat a square 8-inch baking pan with nonstick cooking spray.

2. Place the flour, baking powder, ginger, cinnamon, cloves, nutmeg, and salt in a mixing bowl and whisk to combine. Set the mixture aside.

3. Combine the molasses and stout in a small saucepan and bring to a simmer over medium heat. Remove the pan from heat and whisk in the baking soda. Set the mixture aside.

4. In the work bowl of a stand mixer fitted with the paddle attachment, beat the eggs, sugar, dark brown sugar, and canola oil until the mixture is light and fluffy, about 5 minutes. Add the molasses mixture, beat until incorporated, and then add the dry mixture.

5. Reduce the speed to low and beat until the resulting mixture comes together as a smooth batter.

6. Pour the batter into the prepared pan, place it in the oven, and bake until a cake tester inserted into the center of the bread comes out clean, 50 to 60 minutes.

7. Remove the pan from the oven and place it on a wire rack. Let the bread cool completely.

8. Remove the bread from the pan and spread ganache all over the exterior. Sprinkle confectioners' sugar over the top and let the chocolate set before slicing and serving.

Challah

Yield: 1 Loaf ◆ Active Time: 1 Hour ◆ Total Time: 5 Hours

1½ cups lukewarm water (90°F)

1 tablespoon plus 2 teaspoons active dry yeast

4 eggs, 1 beaten

¼ cup extra-virgin olive oil

29¾ oz. bread flour, plus more as needed

¼ cup sugar

1½ tablespoons fine sea salt

½ cup chopped dates

Slivered almonds, for topping

1. Place the water and yeast in the work bowl of a stand mixer and gently whisk to combine. Let the mixture sit until it starts to foam, about 10 minutes.

2. Fit the mixer with the dough hook, add the 3 unbeaten eggs, oil, flour, sugar, and salt to the work bowl, and work the mixture on low until it comes together as a dough, about 2 minutes.

3. Raise the speed to medium and knead until the dough becomes elastic and starts to pull away from the side of the bowl, about 6 minutes. Add the dates and work the dough until they are evenly distributed.

4. Cover the mixing bowl with a kitchen towel, place it in a naturally warm spot, and let the dough rise until it has doubled in size.

5. Place the dough on a flour-dusted work surface and punch it down. Divide the dough into four pieces that are each 12.7 oz.

6. Shape each piece into an oval, cover the pieces with linen towels, and let them rest for 15 to 30 minutes.

7. Preheat the oven to 350°F. Line a baking sheet with parchment paper.

8. Using the palms of your hands, gently roll the dough into strands that are about 2 feet long.

9. Take the strands and fan them out so that one end of each of them is touching. Press down on the ends where they are touching.

10. Take the right-most strand (Strand 1) and cross it over to the left so that it is horizontal. Take the left-most strand (Strand 2) and cross it over to the right so that it is horizontal.

11. Move Strand 1 between the two strands that have yet to move. Move the strand to the right of Strand 1 to the left so that it is horizontal. This will be known as Strand 3.
12. Move Strand 2 between Strand 1 and Strand 4. Move Strand 4 to the right so that it is horizontal.
13. Repeat moving the horizontal strands to the middle and replacing them with the opposite, outer strands until the entire loaf is braided. Pinch the ends of the loaf together and tuck them under the bread.
14. Carefully transfer the bread to the baking sheet. Brush the dough with the beaten egg and sprinkle the almonds over the bread.
15. Place the bread in the oven and bake until it is golden brown and the internal temperature is at least 210°F, about 30 minutes.
16. Remove the challah from the oven, place it on a wire rack, and let it cool completely before slicing and serving.

Challah, see page 156

For the Sponge

½ cup whole milk, warmed

4½ teaspoons active dry yeast

2 tablespoons honey

4 oz. bread flour

For the Dough

5 eggs, 1 beaten

2 oz. sugar

1 lb. bread flour

2 teaspoons fine sea salt

4 oz. unsalted butter, softened

Confectioners' sugar, for topping

Holiday Brioche

Yield: 1 Loaf ◆ Active Time: 45 Minutes ◆ Total Time: 4 Hours

1. To prepare the sponge, place all of the ingredients in the work bowl of a stand mixer and stir to combine. Cover it with plastic wrap and let the mixture sit until it starts to bubble, about 30 minutes.
2. To begin preparations for the dough, add the 4 unbeaten eggs to the sponge and whisk to incorporate.
3. Add the sugar, flour, and salt, fit the mixer with the dough hook, and work the mixture on low for 5 minutes.
4. Over the course of 2 minutes, add the butter a little at a time with the mixer running. When all of the butter has been added, knead the mixture on low for 5 minutes.
5. Raise the speed to medium and knead the dough until it begins to pull away from the side of the work bowl, about 6 minutes. Cover the bowl with a kitchen towel, place the dough in a naturally warm spot, and let it rise until it has doubled in size, about 1 hour.
6. Preheat the oven to 350°F. Line a baking sheet with nonstick cooking spray. Divide the dough into four equal pieces and roll each one into a large, thin circle. Stack the pieces of dough on top of one another and place the stack on top of a piece of parchment paper.
7. Place a 3-inch circular object in the center of the stack, and cut the dough into 16 equal pieces. Working around the dough, take two strands and twist them away from one another two times. Pinch the ends to join the two strands together.
8. Use the parchment paper to lift up the brioche and place it on the baking sheet. Cover the pan with plastic wrap and let it rise for 30 minutes.
9. Brush the brioche with the beaten egg, place it in the oven, and bake until it is golden brown and the internal temperature is at least 200°F, 35 to 45 minutes.
10. Remove the brioche from the oven, place it on a wire rack, and let it cool completely. If desired, dust the brioche with confectioners' sugar before serving.

Winter Harvest Loaf

Yield: 1 Loaf ◆ Active Time: 45 Minutes ◆ Total Time: 4 Hours

1. Place the water in the work bowl of a stand mixer. Sprinkle the yeast over the water, gently whisk to combine, and let the mixture sit for 10 minutes.

2. Add the unbeaten egg, egg yolk, olive oil, sugar, and molasses and fit the mixer with the dough hook. Add the flour, cocoa powder, millet seeds, rolled oats, caraway seeds, fennel seeds, and salt. Work the mixture on low until it just starts to come together as a dough, about 1 minute.

3. Raise the speed to medium and work the dough until it comes away clean from the side of the work bowl and is elastic, about 6 minutes.

4. Spray a mixing bowl with nonstick cooking spray. Transfer the dough to a flour-dusted work surface and knead it until it is extensible.

5. Shape the dough into a ball, place it in the bowl, and cover the bowl with a kitchen towel. Place the dough in a naturally warm spot and let it rise until it has doubled in size, 1 to 2 hours.

6. Place the dough on a flour-dusted work surface and shape it into a tight round. Place the dough on a piece of parchment paper, seam side down.

7. Cover the dough with a kitchen towel, place it in a naturally warm spot, and let it rise until it has doubled in size.

8. Preheat the oven to 350°F. Place a Dutch oven in the oven as it warms.

9. Brush the dough with the beaten egg. Using a very sharp knife, score the top of the dough for its entire length. Top the dough with additional oats.

10. Remove the Dutch oven from the oven. Use the parchment paper to lift the dough and then carefully lower it into the Dutch oven. Cover the Dutch oven and place it back in the oven.

11. Bake the bread for 20 minutes, uncover the Dutch oven, and bake the bread until it is golden brown and the internal temperature is at least 200°F, 35 to 45 minutes.

12. Remove the bread from the oven, place it on a wire rack, and let it cool completely before slicing.

6 oz. lukewarm water (90°F)

1 tablespoon active dry yeast

2 eggs, 1 beaten

1 egg yolk

1 oz. extra-virgin olive oil

1 oz. sugar

1 tablespoon molasses

12¾ oz. bread flour, plus more as needed

4 teaspoons cocoa powder

½ cup millet seeds

¼ cup rolled oats, plus more for topping

2 tablespoons caraway seeds, toasted

1 tablespoon fennel seeds, toasted

2 teaspoons kosher salt

For the Filling

1 cup unsalted butter, softened

8 oz. sugar, plus more to taste

8 oz. dark brown sugar

1 teaspoon pure vanilla extract

2 tablespoons cinnamon

For the Glaze

1 lb. confectioners' sugar

4 oz. water

1 teaspoon pure vanilla extract

Pinch of kosher salt

For the Dough

12 oz. lukewarm water (90°F)

1 tablespoon plus 2 teaspoons active dry yeast

3 eggs

¼ cup extra-virgin olive oil

2 lbs. bread flour, plus more as needed

¼ cup sugar, plus more to taste

1½ tablespoons fine sea salt

Cinnamon Buns

Yield: 12 Rolls ◇ Active Time: 1 Hour ◇ Total Time: 4 Hours and 30 Minutes

1. To prepare the filling, place all of the ingredients in the work bowl of a stand mixer fitted with a paddle attachment and beat on medium until the mixture is light and fluffy. Transfer to a mixing bowl and set aside. Wipe out the work bowl.

2. To prepare the glaze, place all of the ingredients in a mixing bowl and whisk to combine. Cover it with plastic wrap and set it aside.

3. To begin preparations for the dough, place the water and yeast in the work bowl of the stand mixer, gently stir, and let the mixture sit until foamy, about 10 minutes.

4. Add the eggs, oil, flour, sugar, and salt, fit the mixer with the dough hook, and work the mixture on low until the dough starts to come together, about 2 minutes. Raise the speed to medium and knead until the dough is elastic and pulls away from the side of the bowl. Cover the bowl with plastic wrap, place it in a naturally warm spot, and allow the dough to rise until it has doubled in size.

5. Turn the dough out onto a flour-dusted work surface. Use a rolling pin to roll the dough into a rectangle that is about 24 x 12 inches.

6. Spread the filling evenly across the dough, leaving an inch of dough uncovered on the wide side closest to yourself. Sprinkle sugar lightly over the filling. This will help provide friction and allow for a tight roll.

7. Take the side farthest away and roll the dough into a tight spiral. Pinch the seam to seal the roll closed. Cut the roll into twelve 2-inch-wide pieces.

8. Spray a large, rectangular baking dish with nonstick cooking spray. Place the buns in the pan in an even layer. Cover the rolls with plastic wrap, place them in a naturally warm spot, and let them rise until they have doubled in size.

9. Preheat the oven to 350°F.

10. Place the buns in the oven and bake until their internal temperature is 210°F, 20 to 30 minutes.

11. Remove the buns from the oven and spread the glaze over the top. Let them cool slightly before serving.

Pumpkin Sticky Buns

Yield: 12 Buns   ◆   Active Time: 1 Hour   ◆   Total Time: 4 Hours and 30 Minutes

1. To prepare the filling, place all of the ingredients in the work bowl of a stand mixer fitted with the paddle attachment and beat until the mixture is light and fluffy. Transfer the filling to a mixing bowl and set aside. Wipe out the work bowl.

2. To prepare the glaze, place all of the ingredients in a mixing bowl and whisk to combine. Cover it with plastic wrap and set it aside.

3. To begin preparations for the dough, place the milk and yeast in the work bowl, gently stir, and let the mixture sit until it is foamy, about 10 minutes.

4. Add the melted butter, egg, egg yolk, and pumpkin puree and whisk to combine. Fit the mixer with the dough hook, add the flour, dark brown sugar, and salt, and work the mixture on low until the dough starts to come together, about 2 minutes. Raise the speed to medium and knead until the dough is elastic and pulls away from the side of the bowl.

5. Place the dough on a flour-dusted work surface, form it into a ball, and return it to the work bowl. Cover the bowl with plastic wrap, place it in a naturally warm spot, and let the dough to rise until it has doubled in size.

6. Spread 1 cup of the filling over the bottom of a 13 x 9-inch baking pan.

7. Turn the dough out onto a flour-dusted work surface. Use a rolling pin to roll the dough into a rectangle that is about 24 x 12 inches.

8. Spread the remaining filling evenly over the dough, leaving an inch of dough uncovered on the wide side closest to yourself.

9. Take the dough by the wide side farthest away from you and roll it into a tight spiral. Pinch the seam to seal the roll closed.

10. Cut the roll into twelve 2-inch-wide buns.

11. Place the 12 buns in the pan in an even layer. Cover them with plastic wrap, place them in a naturally warm spot, and let them rise until doubled in size.

12. Preheat the oven to 350°F.

13. Place the buns in the oven and bake until they are golden brown and their internal temperature is at least 210°F, 20 to 30 minutes.

14. Remove the buns from the oven and spread the glaze over the top. Let them cool slightly before serving.

For the Filling

1 cup unsalted butter, softened

8 oz. sugar

8 oz. dark brown sugar

1 teaspoon pure vanilla extract

2 tablespoons cinnamon

1 tablespoon freshly grated nutmeg

1 teaspoon ground ginger

1 teaspoon cardamom

½ teaspoon ground cloves

For the Glaze

1 lb. confectioners' sugar

4 oz. water

1 teaspoon pure vanilla extract

Pinch of kosher salt

For the Dough

1 cup milk, warmed

1 tablespoon active dry yeast

4 oz. unsalted butter, melted

1 egg

1 egg yolk

6 oz. pumpkin puree

24 oz. bread flour, plus more as needed

2 oz. dark brown sugar

1½ teaspoons fine sea salt

Sourdough Bread

Yield: 1 Loaf ◆ Active Time: 1 Hour and 30 Minutes ◆ Total Time: 24 Hours

1 cup water, at room temperature

14.1 oz. bread flour, plus more as needed

1.3 oz. whole wheat flour

8 oz. Sourdough Starter (see page 270)

2 teaspoons kosher salt

1. Place the water and flours in the work bowl of a stand mixer fitted with the dough hook and work the mixture at low speed for 6 minutes. Remove the bowl from the mixer and cover it with plastic wrap. Let the dough sit at room temperature for 1 hour to allow the dough to autolyse.

2. Place the work bowl back on the mixer and add the starter and salt. Knead the mixture at low speed until the dough starts to come together, about 2 minutes. Increase the speed to medium and knead until the dough is elastic and pulls away from the side of the bowl.

3. Dust a 9-inch banneton (proofing basket) with flour. Shape the dough into a ball and place it in the proofing basket, seam side down. Cover the bread with plastic wrap and let rise on the counter for 2 hours.

4. Place the proofing basket in the refrigerator and let it rest overnight.

5. Preheat the oven to 450°F and place a baking stone on a rack positioned in the middle.

6. Dust a peel with flour and gently turn the bread onto the peel so that the seam is facing up.

7. Using a very sharp knife, carefully score the dough just off center, making sure the knife is at a 45-degree angle to the dough.

8. Gently slide the sourdough onto the baking stone. Spray the oven with 5 spritzes of water and bake the bread for 20 minutes.

9. Open the oven, spray the oven with 5 more spritzes of water, and bake until the bread is golden brown and the internal temperature of the bread is at least 210°F, about 20 minutes.

10. Remove the bread from the oven, place it on a wire rack, and let it cool completely before slicing.

BREADS & BREAKFAST TREATS

Chocolate Babka

Yield: 2 Loaves ⋄ Active Time: 45 Minutes ⋄ Total Time: 4 Hours

1. To prepare the filling, fill a small saucepan halfway with water and bring it to a gentle simmer. In a heatproof bowl, combine the dark chocolate and butter. Place the bowl over the simmering water and stir until the mixture is melted and smooth. Remove the bowl from heat, add the confectioners' sugar and cocoa powder, and whisk until thoroughly combined. Set the mixture aside.

2. To begin preparations for the dough, whisk together the water, yeast, eggs, and olive oil in the work bowl of a stand mixer fitted with the dough hook. Add the flour, sugar, and salt and work the mixture on low for 1 minute. Raise the speed to medium and knead the mixture until it comes together as a dough and pulls away from the side of the bowl.

3. Place the dough on a flour-dusted work surface, form it into a ball, and return it to the work bowl. Cover it with plastic wrap and let it rise until doubled in size.

4. Turn the dough out onto a flour-dusted work surface and divide it in half. Use a rolling pin to roll each piece into a rectangle that is about 8 x 6 inches.

5. Spread ½ cup of the filling evenly across the pieces of dough, leaving an inch of dough uncovered on the wide side closest to yourself.

6. Take the wide side farthest away from you and roll the pieces of dough into tight spirals. Using a bench scraper, cut the rolls of dough in half lengthwise. Turn the rolls of dough so that the centers are facing out. Carefully twist the dough to form 3 full turns. Pinch the ends to seal.

7. Coat two 8 x 4-inch loaf pans with nonstick cooking spray and place a piece of dough in each one.

8. Cover the loaves with plastic wrap and let them rise until they crest above the edges of the pans. Preheat the oven to 350°F.

9. Place the loaves in the oven and bake until they are golden brown and their internal temperature is at least 210°F, 45 to 55 minutes.

10. Remove from the oven and transfer the babka to a wire rack. Let them cool completely before serving.

For the Filling

6 oz. dark chocolate (55 to 65 percent)

6 oz. unsalted butter

3 oz. confectioners' sugar

2 oz. cocoa powder

For the Dough

1½ cups lukewarm water (90°F)

1 tablespoon plus 2 teaspoons active dry yeast

3 eggs

¼ cup extra-virgin olive oil

2 lbs. bread flour, plus more as needed

¼ cup sugar

1½ tablespoons kosher salt

Pannettone

Yield: 3 Panettone ◆ Active Time: 3 Hours ◆ Total Time: 2 to 3 Days

For the Pasta Madre

½ oz. Sourdough Starter (see page 270)

Water, as needed

All-purpose flour, as needed

For the First Dough

3½ oz. egg yolks

1 cup water

16.9 oz. strong bread flour or panettone flour

3½ oz. sugar

6.3 oz. pasta madre

4.3 oz. unsalted butter, chopped, plus more as needed

For the Second Dough

8½ oz. strong bread flour or panettone flour

6.7 oz. egg yolks

⅓ oz. powdered milk

1 (scant) teaspoon barley malt

1.2 oz. honey

1 teaspoon orange extract

Seeds of 2 vanilla beans

2 (scant) teaspoons fine sea salt

4.9 oz. sugar

4 oz. unsalted butter, chopped, plus more as needed

5 oz. diced candied orange peels

5 oz. chopped candied citrus peels

10 oz. raisins

1. Begin preparations for the pasta madre 2 to 3 days before you are going to start baking. Combine the starter with 1¾ oz. water and 3½ oz. flour in a large bowl. Cover the bowl with plastic wrap and let it rest for 12 hours.

2. Combine 1¾ oz. of the pasta madre with 1¾ oz. water and 3½ oz. flour.

3. Perform three feedings of the pasta madre, one every 3 to 4 hours. The fed starter should be kept in a naturally warm spot, ideally about 79°F. The schedule should look like this: first feeding (morning): 1¾ oz. of the stiff starter with 1¾ oz. water and 3½ oz. flour; second feeding (lunchtime): 3½ oz. stiff starter, 1¾ oz. water and 3½ oz. flour; final feeding (late afternoon): 3½ oz. stiff starter, 1¾ oz. water and 3½ oz. flour.

4. To begin preparations for the first dough, place the egg yolks and water in the work bowl of a stand mixer fitted with the paddle attachment and beat to combine. Fit the mixer with the dough hook, add the flour and sugar, and work the mixture on low until combined. Gradually add the pasta madre and knead to incorporate.

5. Add the butter in three increments and knead the dough for about 6 minutes on low if using a stand mixer. The first dough should be mixed for no more than 10 minutes after the flour has been added.

THE CHRISTMAS BAKING COOKBOOK

6. Place the dough in a deep bowl and let the the dough rise at room temperature until it is 3 to 4 times its original size, 10 to 12 hours.

7. To begin preparations for the second dough, place the first dough and two-thirds of the flour in the work bowl of a stand mixer fitted with the dough hook and mix on low speed for 2 minutes. Add the egg yolks and the remaining flour and knead on medium speed for about 2 minutes.

8. Add the powdered milk and malt and mix for 1 minute. Add the honey, orange extract, vanilla seeds, and salt and mix for 1 minute. Add the sugar and mix at medium-high speed until the sugar is fully dissolved and the dough sticks to the hook, 2 to 5 minutes.

9. Gradually add the butter and work the dough at medium speed until it wraps tightly around the hook and is elastic, about 10 minutes. Add the candied peels and raisins and work the dough until they are evenly distributed.

10. Let the dough rest in the mixing bowl for 30 minutes.

11. Coat a work surface with butter and place the dough on it. Shape the dough into 3 tight balls that are each 30 oz. and place them in three 26 oz. panettone molds.

12. Place the panettone molds on baking sheets. Let the rounds rise in a naturally warm spot until the dough reaches the edges of the molds, 5 to 10 hours.

13. Preheat the oven to 350°F. Gently score a cross on top of each panettone and slightly pull up on the edges of each cross. Ideally you want to perform a scarpatura, detaching the edges from the dough with a razor, but if you are making your first attempt at making panettone, just place a small piece of butter in the center of each cross, on top of the panettone.

14. Place the panettone in the oven and bake until their internal temperature is around 200°F, 35 to 45 minutes. Do not open the oven until at least 35 minutes have passed.

15. Remove the panettone from the oven, put 2 skewers in the bottom part of the panettone, and flip them upside down. Hang the panettone by the skewers and let them remain upside down until cool, 2 to 3 hours.

16. Spray fitted cellophane sheets with grain alcohol and wrap the panettone with them. Stored this way, the panettone will keep for several weeks.

Lemon & Ginger Scones

Yield: 10 Scones ◊ Active Time: 15 Minutes ◊ Total Time: 1 Hour and 15 Minutes

- 3 eggs
- 5 oz. heavy cream
- 1 lb. all-purpose flour
- 3 oz. sugar
- 8 oz. unsalted butter, chilled and cubed
- 1½ tablespoons baking powder
- 1½ teaspoons kosher salt
- Zest of 2 lemons
- 2 cups diced crystallized ginger
- Royal Icing (see page 264), for topping

1. Line a baking sheet with parchment paper.
2. Place the eggs and 3 oz. of heavy cream in a measuring cup and whisk to combine. Set the mixture aside.
3. Place the flour, sugar, butter, baking powder, salt, and lemon zest in the work bowl of a stand mixer fitted with the paddle attachment and beat the mixture until it comes together as a crumbly dough, with the butter reduced to pea-sized pieces. Take care not to overmix the dough.
4. Transfer the dough to a mixing bowl, add the egg mixture and ginger, and gently fold the mixture until it is a smooth batter.
5. Drop 4 oz. portions of the batter onto the baking sheet, making sure to leave enough space between them. Brush the top of each portion with the remaining cream.
6. Place the scones in the refrigerator and chill for 20 minutes. Preheat the oven to 375°F.
7. Place the pan in the oven and bake until they are golden brown and a cake tester inserted into the center of each scone comes out clean, 22 to 25 minutes.
8. Remove from the oven and place the pan on a wire rack. Let the scones cool slightly before topping them with icing and serving.

Orange Spice Muffins

Yield: 12 Muffins ◇ Active Time: 20 Minutes ◇ Total Time: 1 Hour

17 oz. all-purpose flour

1 tablespoon baking powder

1½ teaspoons kosher salt

2 teaspoons cinnamon

Pinch of freshly grated nutmeg

½ teaspoon ground cloves

8 oz. unsalted butter, softened

10 oz. sugar

Zest of 2 oranges

6 eggs

½ cup sour cream

11 oz. milk

½ cup walnuts, chopped

Confectioners' sugar, for dusting

1. Preheat the oven to 375°F. Line a 12-well muffin pan with paper liners.

2. Place the flour, baking powder, salt, cinnamon, nutmeg, and cloves in a mixing bowl and whisk to combine. Set the mixture aside.

3. In the work bowl of a stand mixer fitted with the paddle attachment, cream the butter, sugar, and orange zest on medium until the mixture is light and fluffy, about 5 minutes. Add the eggs and beat to incorporate. Add the dry mixture, reduce the speed to low, and beat until the resulting mixture comes together as a smooth batter. Add the sour cream and beat until incorporated. Gradually add the milk and beat to incorporate. Add the walnuts, reduce the speed to low, and beat until evenly distributed.

4. Pour ½ cup of muffin batter into each well and place the pan in the oven. Bake the muffins until a cake tester inserted into the center of each one comes out clean, 20 to 25 minutes.

5. Remove the muffins from the oven, place the pan on a wire rack, and let the muffins cool completely. Sprinkle confectioners' sugar over the top and serve.

Cinnamon Babka

Yield: 2 Loaves ◆ Active Time: 45 Minutes ◆ Total Time: 4 Hours

1. To prepare the filling, place all of the ingredients in a mixing bowl and whisk until thoroughly combined. Set the mixture aside.

2. To begin preparations for the dough, whisk together the water, yeast, eggs, and olive oil in the work bowl of a stand mixer fitted with the dough hook. Add the flour, sugar, and salt and work the mixture on low for 1 minute. Raise the speed to medium and knead the mixture until it comes together as a dough and pulls away from the side of the bowl.

3. Place the dough on a flour-dusted work surface, form it into a ball, and return it to the work bowl. Cover it with plastic wrap and let it rise until doubled in size.

4. Turn the dough out onto a flour-dusted work surface and divide it in half. Use a rolling pin to roll each piece into a rectangle that is about 8 x 6 inches.

5. Spread ½ cup of the filling evenly across the pieces of dough, leaving an inch of dough uncovered on the wide side closest to yourself.

6. Take the wide side farthest away from you and roll the pieces of dough into tight spirals. Using a bench scraper, cut the rolls of dough in half lengthwise. Turn the rolls of dough so that the centers are facing out. Carefully twist the dough to form 3 full turns. Pinch the ends to seal.

7. Coat two 8 x 4-inch loaf pans with nonstick cooking spray and place a piece of dough in each one.

8. Cover the loaves with plastic wrap and let them rise until they crest above the edges of the pans. Preheat the oven to 350°F.

9. Place the loaves in the oven and bake until they are golden brown and their internal temperature is at least 210°F, 45 to 55 minutes.

10. Remove from the oven and transfer the babka to a wire rack. Let them cool completely before serving.

For the Filling

7 oz. light brown sugar

1 tablespoon ground cinnamon

½ teaspoon finely grated orange zest

¼ teaspoon fine sea salt

For the Dough

1½ cups lukewarm water (90°F)

1 tablespoon plus 2 teaspoons active dry yeast

3 eggs

¼ cup extra-virgin olive oil

2 lbs. bread flour, plus more as needed

¼ cup sugar

1½ tablespoons kosher salt

Cinnamon Twists, see page 192

Pastries

When it comes to Christmas desserts, cookies are the workhorses, able to be turned out in batches large enough to soothe the ceaseless cravings that seem to arise during the holiday season. Cakes are the showstoppers, the treats that are greeted with oohs and ahs. But the preparations in this chapter are those that will get the most people excited, because, while undeniably decadent, pastries maintain a stunning lightness—it always feels possible to indulge just a bit more when a pastry is the confection under consideration.

Combine that rare power with their eye-catching appearance, and having a few pastries on the dessert table is a must if you want to master the art of Christmas baking.

Apple Strudel

Yield: 6 Servings ♦ Active Time: 25 Minutes ♦ Total Time: 1 Hour and 30 Minutes

¾ lb. apples, peeled, cores removed, chopped

¼ teaspoon lemon zest

1 teaspoon fresh lemon juice

1½ tablespoons sugar

Dash of cinnamon

¼ teaspoon ground ginger

2 pinches of fine sea salt

4 tablespoons unsalted butter, melted

7 sheets of frozen phyllo dough, thawed

1 tablespoon confectioners' sugar, plus more for dusting

1. Preheat the oven to 350°F and line a baking sheet with parchment paper. Place the apples, lemon zest, lemon juice, sugar, cinnamon, ginger, and a pinch of salt in a large mixing bowl and toss until the apples are evenly coated. Place the mixture in a skillet and cook over medium heat until the apples begin to release their liquid. Remove the pan from heat and let it cool for 10 minutes before draining the mixture.

2. Place the melted butter in a bowl and stir in the remaining salt.

3. Brush a sheet of phyllo dough with some of the salted butter and lightly dust it with some of the confectioners' sugar. Repeat with the remaining sheets of phyllo dough, stacking them on top of one another after they have been dressed.

4. Place the apple mixture in the center of the phyllo sheets, leaving a 2-inch border of dough on the sides. Fold the border over the filling so that the edges overlap and gently press down to seal.

5. Place the strudel on the baking sheet, place it in the oven, and bake, rotating the sheet halfway through, until the strudel is golden brown, 30 to 40 minutes. Remove the strudel from the oven, transfer it to a cutting board, and let it cool slightly. Slice the strudel into the desired portions and dust with additional confectioners' sugar before serving.

Struffoli

Yield: 60 Struffoli ◆ Active Time: 40 Minutes ◆ Total Time: 2 Hours

14.1 oz. all-purpose flour, plus more as needed

1.4 oz. sugar

1 teaspoon fine sea salt

3 eggs

2.8 oz. unsalted butter

Zest of 1 orange

Zest of 1 lemon

1½ tablespoons rum or anise liqueur

Extra-virgin olive oil, as needed

1 (scant) cup honey

¼ cup confectioners' sugar

Colored sugar sprinkles, for topping

1. Place the flour, sugar, and salt in a mixing bowl and stir to combine. Add the eggs and work the mixture until they have been incorporated.

2. Add the butter, orange zest, lemon zest, and rum or anise liqueur and work the mixture until it comes together as a smooth dough. Cover the dough with plastic wrap and chill it in the refrigerator for 1 hour.

3. Place the dough on a flour-dusted work surface, flatten it slightly, and cut it into ½-inch-thick strips. Roll the strips into long, thin logs, cut each log into ½-inch-long pieces, and shape the pieces into rounds.

4. Add olive oil to a narrow, deep, heavy-bottomed saucepan with high edges until it is 2 inches deep and warm it to 340°F. Add a handful of struffoli at a time and fry until they are just golden brown, about 1 minute. Remove the fried struffoli with a slotted spoon and place them on a paper towel-lined plate to drain.

5. Place the honey and confectioners' sugar in a saucepan and warm the mixture over low heat until the honey has liquefied.

6. Add all of the struffoli to the pan and gently stir until they are all coated.

7. Pile the struffoli on a serving dish or arrange them in a circle. Top with sugar sprinkles and serve.

Beigli

Yield: 2 Beigli ◆ Active Time: 30 Minutes ◆ Total Time: 24 Hours

For the Dough

5.3 oz. lukewarm sour cream (90°F)

2/3 oz. instant yeast

1 tablespoon confectioners' sugar

17.6 oz. all-purpose flour

8.8. oz. unsalted butter

Pinch of fine sea salt

2 eggs, separated

For the Filling

1½ cups poppy seeds

1¾ cups confectioners' sugar

5 oz. water

⅓ cup raisins

Zest and juice of 1 lemon

1. To begin preparations for the dough, place the sour cream, yeast, and confectioners' sugar in a bowl and gently stir to combine. Set the mixture aside.

2. Place the flour, butter, and salt in a mixing bowl and work the mixture with a pastry cutter until it comes together as a crumbly dough. Add the sour cream mixture and knead until the resulting mixture comes together as a smooth dough. Cover the dough with plastic wrap and chill it in the refrigerator overnight.

3. To prepare the filling, place all of the ingredients in a food processor and pulse until well combined. Set the filling aside.

4. Line a baking sheet with parchment paper. Place the dough on a flour-dusted work surface and divide it into two pieces. Roll them out into ¼-inch-thick rectangles and spread the filling over the top, leaving a 1-inch border at the side closest to you. Working from the opposite side, roll the pieces of dough up tightly and place them on the baking sheet.

5. Place the egg yolks in a bowl and beat them. Brush the beigli with the egg yolks and let them rest for 30 minutes.

6. Preheat the oven to 350°F. Brush the beigli with the egg whites and place them in the oven. Bake until the tops are golden brown, about 40 minutes.

7. Remove the beigli from the oven and let them cool before slicing and serving.

Sopaipillas

Yield: 24 Sopaipillas ◆ Active Time: 35 Minutes ◆ Total Time: 1 Hour

12 oz. self-rising flour

1½ teaspoons baking powder

1 teaspoon fine sea salt

1 teaspoon sugar

1 cup warm water (105°F)

Canola oil, as needed

Confectioners' sugar, for dusting

Cinnamon, for dusting

Honey, for serving

1. In the bowl of a stand mixer fitted with the whisk attachment, combine the flour, baking powder, salt, and sugar. Turn the mixer on low speed and slowly drizzle in the warm water. Beat until the mixture comes together as a soft, smooth dough. Cover the bowl with a kitchen towel and let the dough rest for 20 minutes.

2. Add canola oil to a Dutch oven until it is about 2 inches deep and warm it to 325°F. Line a baking sheet with paper towels and place it beside the stove.

3. Divide the dough in half and pat each piece into a rectangle. Cut each rectangle into 12 squares and roll each square to ⅛ inch thick.

4. Working in batches of three, place the sopaipillas in the oil and use a pair of tongs to gently submerge them until puffy and golden brown, about 1 minute. Transfer the fried pastries to the baking sheet to drain and cool. When all of the sopaipillas have been fried, dust them with confectioners' sugar and cinnamon and serve with honey.

Sufganiyot

Yield: 20 Sufganiyot ◆ Active Time: 45 Minutes ◆ Total Time: 3 Hours

3½ tablespoons unsalted butter, chopped, plus more as needed

3½ cups all-purpose flour, plus more as needed

½ teaspoon fine sea salt

¼ cup sugar

1 tablespoon instant yeast

1 egg

1¼ cups lukewarm milk (85°F)

Avocado oil, as needed

½ cup strawberry jam

¼ cup confectioners' sugar, for dusting

1. Coat a mixing bowl with some butter and set it aside. Sift the flour into the work bowl of a stand mixer fitted with the dough hook. Add the salt, sugar, and yeast and stir to incorporate.

2. Add the egg and butter to the mixture and mix to incorporate. Gradually add the milk and work the mixture until it comes together as a soft dough, 8 to 10 minutes.

3. Form the dough into a ball and place it in the buttered mixing bowl. Cover with a linen towel and let it rise until doubled in size, about 2 hours.

4. Line two baking sheets with parchment paper. Place the dough on a flour-dusted work surface and roll it out until it is about ¾ inch thick. Cut the dough into 2-inch circles, place them on the baking sheets, and cover with a linen towel. Let them rise for another 20 minutes.

5. Add avocado oil to a cast-iron Dutch oven until it is about 2 inches deep and warm it to 325°F. Add the dough in batches of four and fry until golden brown, about 6 minutes, turning them over halfway through.

6. Drain the sufganiyot on a paper towel-lined plate. Fill a piping bag with the jam, and make a small slit on the top of each sufganiyah. Place the piping bag in the slit and fill until you see the filling coming back out. Sprinkle with the confectioners' sugar and enjoy.

Cinnamon Twists

Yield: 24 Twists ♦ Active Time: 15 Minutes ♦ Total Time: 30 Minutes

2 sheets of frozen puff pastry, thawed

1 cup sugar

3½ tablespoons cinnamon

1 teaspoon freshly grated nutmeg

1 egg

1 cup Caramel Sauce (see page 271), warmed, for serving

1. Preheat the oven to 375°F, line a baking sheet with parchment paper, and roll out the sheets of puff pastry. Combine the sugar, cinnamon, and nutmeg in a mixing bowl. Beat the egg in a separate bowl.

2. Lightly brush the top of each pastry sheet with the egg and then sprinkle the sugar-and-spice mixture evenly across both sheets of puff pastry.

3. Cut the pastries into long strips and twist them. Place the strips on the baking sheet and bake until golden brown, 10 to 15 minutes. Remove from the oven, flip each pastry over, and bake for an additional 2 to 3 minutes.

4. Remove the twists from the oven and let them cool until just slightly warm. Serve with the Caramel Sauce on the side.

For the Pastries

17.1 oz. whole milk

1¾ oz. cultured butter, softened

1 vanilla bean

3½ oz. all-purpose flour

7 oz. sugar

Pinch of fine sea salt

2 eggs

2 egg yolks

1¾ oz. dark rum or Cognac

For the Molds

1¾ oz. beeswax

1¾ oz. unsalted butter

Canelés

Yield: 18 Canelés ◆ Active Time: 1 Hour ◆ Total Time: 48 Hours

1. To begin preparations for the pastries, place the milk and butter in a saucepan. Scrape the vanilla bean's seeds into the saucepan, and add the pod as well. Place the pan over medium heat and bring the mixture to a simmer. Immediately remove the pan from heat and let it sit for 10 minutes.

2. In a large mixing bowl, whisk the flour, sugar, and salt together. Set the mixture aside. Place the eggs and egg yolks in a heatproof mixing bowl and whisk to combine, making sure not to add any air to the mixture.

3. While whisking, add the milk mixture in small increments. When all of the milk mixture has been thoroughly incorporated, whisk in the rum or Cognac.

4. Remove the vanilla bean pod and reserve. While whisking, add the tempered eggs to the dry mixture and whisk until just combined, taking care not to overwork the mixture. Strain the custard through a fine sieve. If the mixture is still warm, place the bowl in an ice bath until it has cooled to room temperature.

5. Add the vanilla bean pod to the custard, cover it with plastic wrap, and refrigerate for at least 24 hours; however, 48 hours is strongly recommended.

6. Preheat the oven to 500°F. To prepare the molds, grate the beeswax into a mason jar and add the butter. Place the jar in a saucepan filled with a few inches of water and bring the water to a simmer. When the beeswax mixture is melted and combined, pour it into one mold, immediately pour it back into the jar, and set the mold, right side up, on a wire rack to drain. When all of the molds have been coated, place them in the freezer for 15 minutes. Remove the custard from the refrigerator and let it come to room temperature.

7. Pour the custard into the molds so that they are filled about 85 percent of the way. Place the filled molds, upside down, on a baking sheet, place them in the oven, and bake for 10 minutes. Reduce the oven's temperature to 375°F and bake until they are a deep brown, about 40 minutes. Turn the canelés out onto a wire rack and let them cool completely before enjoying. Reheat the beeswax mixture and let the molds cool before refilling them with the remaining batter.

Flores de Carnaval

Yield: 12 Pastries ◆ Active Time: 20 Minutes ◆ Total Time: 1 Hour

2 cups all-purpose flour, plus more as needed

1 teaspoon baking powder

1 tablespoon sugar, plus more as needed

½ teaspoon kosher salt

2 eggs

1 tablespoon unsalted butter, melted and cooled

1 teaspoon pure vanilla extract

1 tablespoon lemon zest

4.4 oz. whole milk

Canola oil, as needed

Cinnamon, as needed

1. In a large mixing bowl, combine the flour, baking powder, sugar, and salt. Add the eggs, melted butter, vanilla, and lemon zest and work the mixture until it resembles coarse bread crumbs.

2. Gradually incorporate the milk until the mixture comes together as a smooth batter. Cover the mixing bowl with plastic wrap and let it rest for 30 minutes.

3. Add canola oil to a Dutch oven until it is about 2 inches deep and warm it to 350°F.

4. Gently slip the floron—the mold—into the hot oil. Dip the mold into the batter until it is coated and then gently slip it back into the hot oil. The pastry should release from the mold after 1 minute; if it is having trouble releasing, use a wooden spoon to gently remove it from the mold. Fry until the pastry is crispy and golden brown, about 2 minutes.

5. Transfer the pastry to a paper towel-lined plate and let it drain. Repeat with the remaining batter.

6. When all of the pastries have been fried, combine sugar and cinnamon in a shallow bowl. Dredge the pastries in the mixture until coated and serve.

Paris-Brest

Yield: 6 Pastries ◆ Active Time: 50 Minutes ◆ Total Time: 2 Hours

17 oz. water

8½ oz. unsalted butter

1 teaspoon fine sea salt

2.4 oz. sugar

12½ oz. all-purpose flour

7 eggs

1 cup slivered almonds

Hazelnut Mousseline (see page 272)

Confectioners' sugar, for dusting

1. Preheat the oven to 425°F and line two baking sheets with parchment paper. In a medium saucepan, combine the water, butter, salt, and sugar and warm the mixture over medium heat until the butter is melted.

2. Add the flour to the pan and use a rubber spatula or a wooden spoon to fold the mixture until it comes together as a thick, shiny dough, taking care not to let the dough burn.

3. Transfer the dough to the work bowl of a stand mixer fitted with the paddle attachment and beat on medium speed until the dough is no longer steaming and the bowl is just warm to the touch, at least 10 minutes.

4. Incorporate six of the eggs two at a time, scraping down the work bowl between each addition. Transfer the dough to a piping bag fit with an #867 tip (this will be called a "French Star Tip" on occasion). Pipe a 5-inch ring of dough onto a baking sheet and then pipe another ring inside the first ring. Pipe another ring atop the seam between the first two rings. Repeat until all of the dough has been used.

5. In a small bowl, whisk the remaining egg and brush the tops of the dough with it. Arrange the almonds on top and gently press down to ensure they adhere.

6. Place the pastries in the oven and bake for 10 minutes. Lower the oven's temperature to 300°F and bake until golden brown and a cake tester inserted into each one comes out clean, 30 to 35 minutes. Remove from the oven and let them cool on a wire rack.

7. Place the mousseline in a piping bag fit with a plain tip. Using a serrated knife, slice the pastries in half along their equators. Pipe rosettes of the mousseline around the inside. Place the top half of the pastries on top, dust them with confectioners' sugar, and enjoy.

Raspberry Danish

Yield: 20 Danish ◆ Active Time: 30 Minutes ◆ Total Time: 2 Hours

Danish Dough (see page 274)

All-purpose flour, as needed

1¼ cups raspberry jam

1 egg, beaten

Vanilla Glaze (see page 265)

1. Line two baking sheets with parchment paper. Place the dough on a flour-dusted work surface and roll it into a 12-inch square. Using a pizza cutter or chef's knife, slice the dough into twenty 3-inch squares.

2. Working with one square at a time, make four cuts of equal length, starting from the corners and moving toward the center. Make sure to not cut all the way through the center. Make two diagonal cuts about ¼ inch long inside from the edges of the triangles' short sides.

3. Fold the point of every other half toward the center and press down to seal. Place ten danish on each baking sheet. Place 1 tablespoon of jam in the center of each danish.

4. Cover the baking sheets with plastic wrap and let the danish rest at room temperature for 45 minutes.

5. Preheat the oven to 375°F.

6. Brush the danish with the beaten egg, place them in the oven, and bake until they are golden brown, 15 to 20 minutes.

7. Remove the danish from the oven and place them on wire racks to cool for 10 minutes. Brush the tops of the danish with the glaze and let it set before enjoying.

Zeppole

Yield: 4 Servings ◆ Active Time: 30 Minutes ◆ Total Time: 2 Hours

6¼ oz. all-purpose flour

1 tablespoon plus 1 teaspoon baking powder

¼ teaspoon fine sea salt

2 eggs

2 tablespoons sugar

2 cups ricotta cheese

Zest of 1 orange

1 cup milk

1 teaspoon pure vanilla extract

Canola oil, as needed

¼ cup confectioners' sugar, for topping

1. Sift the flour, baking powder, and salt into a bowl. Set the mixture aside.

2. Place the eggs and sugar in a separate bowl and whisk to combine. Add the ricotta, whisk to incorporate, and then stir in the orange zest, milk, and vanilla.

3. Gradually incorporate the dry mixture into the wet mixture until the resulting mixture comes together as a smooth batter. Place the batter in the refrigerator and chill for 1 hour.

4. Add canola oil to a Dutch oven until it is about 2 inches deep and warm it to 350°F. Drop tablespoons of the batter into the hot oil, taking care not to crowd the pot, and fry until the zeppole are golden brown. Transfer the fried zeppole to a paper towel-lined plate and let them drain briefly.

5. To serve, dust the zeppole with confectioners' sugar.

Palmiers

Yield: 16 Palmiers ◆ Active Time: 20 Minutes ◆ Total Time: 2 Hours

1 sheet of frozen puff pastry, thawed

1 cup sugar

¾ teaspoon fine sea salt

1. Place the sheet of puff pastry on a piece of parchment paper. Combine the sugar and salt in a small bowl and sprinkle the mixture over the puff pastry.

2. Working from the edge closest to you, fold puff pastry over itself continually until you get to the center of the sheet. Repeat from the opposite edge.

3. Sandwich the puff pastry together so that it is a log, cover it with plastic wrap, place it in the refrigerator, and chill for 1 hour.

4. Preheat the oven to 375°F. Place a Silpat mat on a baking sheet. Remove the palmier log from the refrigerator and cut it into ¼-inch-wide pieces. Place them on the baking sheet, place the palmiers in the oven, and cook until the tops are golden brown, about 8 minutes.

5. Remove the palmiers from the oven and flip them over. Return them to the oven and bake until golden brown, about 5 minutes.

6. Remove from the oven, transfer the palmiers to wire racks, and let them cool completely before serving.

Churros

Yield: 36 Churros ✧ Active Time: 25 Minutes ✧ Total Time: 30 Minutes

Canola oil, as needed

17.1 oz. milk

40.6 oz. water

1.4 oz. sugar, plus more to taste

0.7 oz. salt

19.4 oz. "00" flour

19.4 oz. all-purpose flour

16 eggs

Cinnamon, to taste

Chocolate Ganache (see page 266), warm, for serving

Caramel Sauce (see page 271), for serving

1. Add canola oil to a Dutch oven until it is about 2 inches deep and warm it to 350°F. Place the milk, water, sugar, and salt in a large saucepan and bring it to a boil.

2. Gradually add the flours and cook, stirring constantly, until the mixture pulls away from the side of the pan.

3. Place the mixture in the work bowl of a stand mixer fitted with the paddle attachment and beat until the dough is almost cool. Incorporate the eggs one at a time, scraping down the work bowl as needed.

4. Combine some cinnamon and sugar in a baking dish and set the mixture aside.

5. Place the dough in a piping bag fitted with a star tip. Pipe 6-inch lengths of dough into the oil and fry until they are golden brown. Place them on paper towel-lined plates to drain and cool slightly. Toss in cinnamon sugar and enjoy, or store the churros in the freezer.

6. To serve frozen churros, preheat the oven to 450°F. Remove the churros from the freezer and toss them in cinnamon sugar until they are coated. Place them in the oven and bake for 5 minutes. Remove them from the oven, toss them in cinnamon sugar again, and serve with the ganache and caramel.

Baklava

Yield: 16 Servings ◆ Active Time: 30 Minutes ◆ Total Time: 1 Hour

- 3½ cups walnuts, toasted
- 17½ oz. sugar
- 1 teaspoon cinnamon
- ¼ teaspoon ground cloves
- 1 lb. frozen phyllo dough, thawed
- 1½ cups unsalted butter, melted
- 1½ cups water
- ½ cup honey
- ½ lemon, sliced thin
- 1 cinnamon stick
- Almonds or hazelnuts, for topping (optional)

1. Place the walnuts, ½ cup of the sugar, cinnamon, and cloves in a food processor. Pulse until very fine and set the mixture aside.

2. Preheat the oven to 375°F and coat a baking pan with non-stick cooking spray. Place the phyllo sheets on a plate and cover with plastic wrap or a damp paper towel to keep them from drying out. Place 1 sheet of phyllo on the pan and brush with some of the melted butter. Repeat with 7 more sheets and spread one-third of the walnut mixture on top. Place 4 more sheets of phyllo dough on top, brushing each with butter. Spread half of the remaining walnut mixture on top, and then repeat. Top the last of the walnut mixture with the remaining sheets of phyllo dough, brushing each one with butter. Trim the edges so that the baklava fits the pan.

3. Cut the pastry into the desired shapes, taking care not to cut through the bottom crust. Place the baklava in the oven and bake until the top layer of phyllo is golden brown, 25 to 30 minutes.

4. While the baklava is in the oven, combine the remaining sugar, water, honey, lemon, and cinnamon stick in a saucepan. Bring to a boil over medium heat while stirring occasionally. Reduce the heat to low and simmer for 5 minutes. Strain the syrup and keep it hot while the baklava finishes baking.

5. Remove the baklava from the oven and pour the hot syrup over the top. Place the pan on a wire rack, let the baklava cool to room temperature, and then cut through the bottom crust. If desired, top with almonds or hazelnuts before serving.

Pumpkin Pie, see page 238

Pies & Tarts

While any time is a good time for pie, that is especially true around Christmas. Any family that views dessert with the proper seriousness undoubtedly counts a pie among the litany of treats that are a staple of their holiday celebrations, and when you consider pie's luscious, comforting nature and its lightness relative to other confections, it's easy to understand why.

You'll find the classic holiday pies—apple, pecan, and pumpkin—here. But you'll also find recipes that cleverly make use of beloved holiday flavors like chocolate truffle, cranberry, and fig, employing pie's versatile and accommodating nature to present old favorites in exciting new packages.

Pecan Pie

Yield: 1 Pie ◇ Active Time: 20 Minutes ◇ Total Time: 1 Hour and 30 Minutes

1 cup light corn syrup

1 cup packed dark brown sugar

3 eggs, lightly beaten

6 tablespoons unsalted butter, melted

½ teaspoon fine sea salt

1 cup pecan halves

1 Perfect Piecrust (see page 276)

All-purpose flour, as needed

1 Preheat the oven to 350°F. Coat a 9-inch pie plate with nonstick cooking spray. Place all of the ingredients, except for the piecrust and flour, in a large mixing bowl and stir to combine. Set the filling aside.

2 Roll out the piecrust on a flour-dusted work surface. Place the dough in the pie plate, trim the edges, and then crimp the crust. Place the crust in the refrigerator for 15 minutes.

3 Pour the filling into the crust. Place the pie in the oven and bake until the crust is golden brown and the filling is set, 45 to 50 minutes. Remove the pie from the oven and let it cool completely before serving.

Apple Pie

Yield: 1 Pie ◆ Active Time: 30 Minutes ◆ Total Time: 1 Hour and 45 Minutes

2 Perfect Piecrusts (see page 276), rolled out

3 Honeycrisp apples, peeled, cored, and sliced

3 Granny Smith apples, peeled, cored, and sliced

½ cup sugar

¼ cup light brown sugar

1½ tablespoons cornstarch

1 teaspoon cinnamon

½ teaspoon freshly grated nutmeg

¼ teaspoon cardamom

Zest and juice of 1 lemon

¼ teaspoon kosher salt

1 egg, beaten

Sanding sugar, for topping

Caramel Sauce (see page 271), for topping (optional)

1 Preheat the oven to 375°F. Coat a 9-inch pie pan with nonstick cooking spray and place one of the crusts in it.

2 Place the apples, sugar, brown sugar, cornstarch, cinnamon, nutmeg, cardamom, lemon juice, lemon zest, and salt in a mixing bowl and toss until the apples are evenly coated.

3 Fill the crust with the apple filling, lay the other crust over the top, and crimp the edge to seal. Brush the top crust with the egg and sprinkle the sanding sugar over it. Cut several slits in the top crust.

4 Place the pie in the oven and bake until the filling is bubbly and has thickened, about 50 minutes.

5 Remove the pie from the oven and let it cool completely. If desired, drizzle caramel over the pie before serving.

THE CHRISTMAS BAKING COOKBOOK

Fig & Pistachio Tart

Yield: 1 Tart ◆ Active Time: 25 Minutes ◆ Total Time: 1 Hour and 15 Minutes

2 cups pistachios

⅔ cup dark brown sugar

1 teaspoon pure vanilla extract

2 egg whites

1 Pâté Sucrée (see page 277), blind baked in a 9-inch tart pan

8 figs, sliced thin

1 Preheat the oven to 350°F. Place 1½ cups of pistachios, the brown sugar, vanilla, and egg whites in a food processor and pulse until the pistachios are finely ground.

2 Pour the mixture into the tart shell and lay the sliced figs over the top. Chop the remaining pistachios and sprinkle them over the tart.

3 Place the tart in the oven and bake until the filling has set and the figs have caramelized, about 30 minutes.

4 Remove the tart from the oven and let it completely before slicing and serving.

Gianduja Whoopie Pies

Yield: 20 Whoopie Pies ◊ Active Time: 30 Minutes ◊ Total Time: 1 Hour

9 oz. all-purpose flour

1½ oz. cocoa powder

1½ teaspoons baking soda

½ teaspoon kosher salt

4 oz. unsalted butter, softened

8 oz. sugar

1 egg

1 teaspoon pure vanilla extract

1 cup buttermilk

2 cups Gianduja Crémeux (see page 279)

1. Preheat the oven to 350°F and line two baking sheets with parchment paper. Sift the flour, cocoa powder, baking soda, and salt into a mixing bowl. Set the mixture aside.

2. In the work bowl of a stand mixer fitted with the paddle attachment, cream the butter and sugar until the mixture is very light and fluffy, about 5 minutes. Scrape down the work bowl with a rubber spatula and then beat the mixture for another 5 minutes.

3. Reduce the speed to low, add the egg, and beat until incorporated. Scrape down the work bowl, raise the speed to medium, and beat the mixture for 1 minute.

4. Reduce the speed to low, add the vanilla and the dry mixture, and beat until the resulting mixture comes together as a smooth batter. Add the buttermilk in a slow stream and beat to incorporate.

5. Scoop 2 oz. portions of the batter onto the baking sheets, making sure to leave 2 inches between each portion. Tap the bottom of the baking sheets gently on the counter to remove any air bubbles and let the portions spread out slightly.

6. Place the pies in the oven and bake until a cake tester inserted into their centers comes out clean, 10 to 12 minutes.

7. Remove the whoopie pies from the oven and let them cool completely on the baking sheets.

8. Carefully remove the whoopie pies from the parchment paper. Scoop about 2 oz. of the crémeux on half of the whoopie pies and then create sandwiches by topping with the remaining half.

For the Crust

24 Oreos

3 oz. unsalted butter, melted

For the Filling

15 Oreos

2 lbs. cream cheese, softened

2/3 cup sugar

1/4 teaspoon kosher salt

4 eggs

1 teaspoon pure vanilla extract

Chocolate Ganache (see page 266), warm

Cookies 'N' Cream Tart

Yield: 1 Tart ⋄ Active Time: 30 Minutes ⋄ Total Time: 8 Hours

1. Preheat the oven to 350°F. To begin preparations for the crust, place the cookies in a food processor and pulse until finely ground. Transfer to a medium bowl and combine with the melted butter.

2. Transfer the mixture to a 9-inch pie plate and press it into the bottom and side in an even layer. Use the bottom of a dry measuring cup to help flatten the bottom of the crust. Use a paring knife to trim away any excess crust and create a flat and smooth edge.

3. Place the pie plate on a baking sheet and bake until it is firm, 8 to 10 minutes. Remove from the oven, transfer the crust to a cooling rack, and let it cool for at least 2 hours.

4. Preheat the oven to 350°F. To begin preparations for the filling, place the cookies in a food processor and pulse until they are finely ground. Set them aside.

5. Bring 8 cups of water to a boil in a small saucepan. In the work bowl of a stand mixer fitted with the paddle attachment, cream the cream cheese, sugar, and salt until the mixture is fluffy, about 10 minutes. Scrape down the sides of the work bowl as needed.

6. Reduce the speed of the mixer to medium and incorporate one egg at a time, scraping down the work bowl as needed. Add the vanilla and beat until incorporated. Remove the work bowl from the mixer and fold in the cookie crumbs.

7. Pour the mixture into the crust, place the tart in a large baking pan with high sides, and gently pour the boiling water into the baking pan until it reaches halfway up the sides of the pie plate. Cover the baking pan with aluminum foil, place it in the oven, and bake until the tart is set and only slightly jiggly in the center, 50 minutes to 1 hour.

8. Turn off the oven and leave the oven door cracked. Allow the tart to rest in the cooling oven for 45 minutes.

9. Remove the tart from the oven and transfer it to a cooling rack. Let it sit at room temperature for 1 hour and then chill it in the refrigerator for 3 hours.

10. Spread the chocolate ganache over the tart and chill it in the refrigerator for another hour before slicing and serving.

Lingonberry Cream Pie

Yield: 1 Pie ◆ Active Time: 15 Minutes ◆ Total Time: 6 Hours and 30 Minutes

For the Crust

24 ginger snaps

3 oz. unsalted butter

For the Filling

8 oz. cream cheese, softened

1⅔ cups sweetened condensed milk

1½ cups Whipped Cream (see page 267)

1 teaspoon pure vanilla extract

1⅓ cups lingonberries

1. Preheat the oven to 350°F. To begin preparations for the crust, place the ginger snaps in a food processor and pulse until finely ground. Transfer to a medium bowl and combine with the melted butter.

2. Transfer the mixture to a 9-inch pie plate and press it into the bottom and side in an even layer. Use the bottom of a dry measuring cup to help flatten the bottom of the crust. Use a paring knife to trim away any excess crust and create a flat and smooth edge.

3. Place the pie plate on a baking sheet and bake until it is firm, 8 to 10 minutes. Remove from the oven, transfer the crust to a cooling rack, and let it cool for at least 2 hours.

4. To begin preparations for the filling, place the cream cheese in the work bowl of a stand mixer fitted with the paddle attachment and beat until smooth and creamy.

5. Add the condensed milk and beat the mixture until it is smooth and thick, about 5 minutes. Remove the bowl from the stand mixer, add the Whipped Cream, vanilla, and lingonberries and fold to incorporate.

6. Spoon the filling into the crust and use a rubber spatula to even out the top. Cover the pie with plastic wrap and freeze until set, about 4 hours.

7. To serve, remove the pie from the freezer and let it sit at room temperature for 10 minutes before slicing.

Nutty Caramel & Cranberry Pie

Yield: 1 Pie ◆ Active Time: 45 Minutes ◆ Total Time: 3 Hours

1 Perfect Piecrust (see page 276), rolled out

1 cup slivered almonds

1 cup cashews, chopped

1⅓ cups sugar

½ cup water

6 tablespoons unsalted butter

1 teaspoon pure vanilla extract

¼ teaspoon kosher salt

1½ cups fresh cranberries

1 Preheat the oven to 375°F. Coat a 9-inch pie plate with nonstick cooking spray and place the piecrust in it.

2 Place the almonds and cashews on a parchment-lined baking sheet, place them in the oven, and toast until they are fragrant and starting to brown, 8 to 10 minutes. Remove from the oven and let them cool. Leave the oven on.

3 In a medium saucepan, bring the sugar and water to a boil over high heat. Cook, swirling the pan occasionally, until the mixture is a deep amber color. Remove the pan from heat.

4 Whisk in the butter, vanilla, and salt and let the caramel cool.

5 Place the toasted nuts and cranberries in a mixing bowl and toss to combine. Place the mixture in the piecrust and pour the caramel over it until the crust is filled. Save any remaining caramel for another preparation.

6 Place the pie in the oven and bake until the filling is set at the edge and the center barely jiggles when you shake the pie plate, about 1 hour. Remove from the oven and let the pie cool completely before slicing and serving.

Squash Whoopie Pies

Yield: 12 Servings ♦ Active Time: 20 Minutes ♦ Total Time: 1 Hour

1⅓ cups all-purpose flour

1 teaspoon cinnamon

1 teaspoon ground ginger

¼ teaspoon ground cloves

½ teaspoon freshly grated nutmeg

½ teaspoon baking soda

½ teaspoon baking powder

1 teaspoon kosher salt

1 cup packed light brown sugar

2 tablespoons real maple syrup

1 cup pureed butternut or acorn squash

1 egg

1 cup extra-virgin olive oil

1⅓ cups confectioners' sugar

¼ cup unsalted butter

8 oz. cream cheese, at room temperature

1-inch piece of fresh ginger, peeled and grated

½ teaspoon pure vanilla extract

1 Preheat the oven to 350°F. Sift the flour, cinnamon, ginger, cloves, nutmeg, baking soda, baking powder, and salt into a mixing bowl.

2 Place the brown sugar, maple syrup, pureed squash, egg, and oil in a separate mixing bowl and stir until combined. Sift the dry mixture into the squash mixture and stir until it has been incorporated.

3 Use an ice cream scoop to place dollops of the batter onto parchment-lined baking sheets. Make sure to leave plenty of space between the scoops. Place the sheets in the oven and bake until the cakes are golden brown, about 10 to 15 minutes. Remove and let cool.

4 While the squash cakes are cooling, place the remaining ingredients in a bowl and beat with a handheld mixer until the mixture is fluffy.

5 When the cakes have cooled completely, spread the filling on one of the cakes. Top with another cake and repeat until all of the cakes and filling have been used.

Cranberry Curd Pie

Yield: 1 Pie ◆ Active Time: 35 Minutes ◆ Total Time: 24 Hours

- 3 cups cranberries
- Juice of 1 orange
- 1¼ cups sugar
- 2 large eggs
- 2 large egg yolks
- 4 oz. unsalted butter, softened
- 1 teaspoon pure vanilla extract
- 1 teaspoon kosher salt
- 1 Graham Cracker Crust (see page 278)
- Whipped Cream (see page 267), for topping

1. Place the cranberries and orange juice in a large saucepan and cook over medium heat, stirring occasionally, until the cranberries start to split, 10 to 15 minutes.

2. Strain the mixture through a fine-mesh sieve into a clean saucepan. Add the sugar, eggs, egg yolks, butter, vanilla, and salt and stir to combine. Cook over low heat, stirring frequently, until the curd thickens, about 10 minutes.

3. Strain the curd into a mixing bowl and let it cool slightly. Preheat the oven to 350°F.

4. Pour the curd into the crust, place the pie in the oven, and bake until the curd is just set, 10 to 12 minutes.

5. Remove the pie from the oven, let it cool completely on a wire rack, and refrigerate overnight before topping with Whipped Cream and serving.

Tarte Tatin

Yield: 1 Tart ◆ Active Time: 1 Hour ◆ Total Time: 50 Hours

6 to 8 Honeycrisp apples, peeled, cores removed, quartered

1⅓ cups all-purpose flour, plus more as needed

¼ cup confectioners' sugar

½ teaspoon fine sea salt

½ cup unsalted butter, chilled

1 egg, beaten

6 tablespoons salted butter, softened

⅔ cup sugar

1 Place the apples in a mixing bowl and let them sit in the refrigerator for 48 hours. This will dry the apples out, keeping the amount of liquid in the tart to a reasonable level.

2 Whisk together the flour, confectioners' sugar, and salt in a large bowl. Add the unsalted butter and use your fingers or a pastry blender to work the mixture until it is a collection of coarse clumps. Add the egg and work the mixture until the dough just holds together. Shape it into a ball and cover it with plastic wrap. Flatten it into a 4-inch disk and refrigerate for 1 hour. If preparing ahead of time, the dough will keep in the refrigerator overnight.

3 Preheat the oven to 375°F. Coat a 10-inch cast-iron skillet with the salted butter and place the pan over low heat. When the butter is melted, remove the skillet from heat and sprinkle the sugar evenly over the butter. Place the apple slices in a circular pattern, starting at the center of the pan and working out to the edge. The pieces should overlap and face the same direction.

4 Place the dough on a flour-dusted work surface and roll it out to ⅛ inch thick. Use the roller to carefully roll up the dough. Place it over the apples and tuck the dough in around the edges.

5 Place the skillet over low heat and gradually raise it until the juices in the pan are a deep amber color, about 7 minutes.

6 Place the skillet in the oven and bake until the crust is golden brown and firm, 35 to 40 minutes.

7 Remove the tart from the oven, let it cool for about 5 minutes, and then run a knife around the edges to loosen the tart. Using oven mitts, carefully invert the tart onto a large plate. Place any apples that are stuck to the skillet back on the tart and enjoy.

Brûléed Buttermilk Pie

Yield: 1 Pie ⋄ Active Time: 10 Minutes ⋄ Total Time: 1 Hour and 30 Minutes

3 large eggs

1 cup plus ⅓ cup sugar

¼ cup honey

3 tablespoons all-purpose flour

4 oz. unsalted butter, melted and slightly cooled

1¼ cups buttermilk

1 teaspoon pure vanilla extract

1 tablespoon fresh lemon juice

1 teaspoon lemon zest

¼ teaspoon kosher salt

1 Perfect Piecrust (see page 276), blind baked

1. Preheat the oven to 350°F. Place all of the ingredients, except for ⅓ cup of sugar and the piecrust, in the work bowl of a stand mixer fitted with the paddle attachment and beat until the mixture is fluffy and thoroughly combined, about 3 to 4 minutes.

2. Pour the mixture into the piecrust, place the pie in the oven, and bake until the filling is set and starting to brown, about 45 minutes.

3. Remove from the oven and let it cool slightly. Spread the remaining sugar evenly over the top, caramelize it with a kitchen torch, and serve.

Chocolate Truffle Pie

Yield: 8 Servings ◆ Active Time: 15 Minutes ◆ Total Time: 2 Hours and 15 Minutes

1½ cups heavy cream

2 cups bittersweet chocolate chips

4 tablespoons unsalted butter, divided into tablespoons

2 tablespoons crème de cacao

1 Perfect Piecrust (see page 276), blind baked

Strawberries, sliced, for topping (optional)

1. Preheat the oven to 350°F. Place the cream in a small saucepan and bring to a boil over medium heat. Place the chocolate chips in a mixing bowl and then pour the boiling cream over the chocolate. Stir until the mixture is smooth, add the butter and crème de cacao, and stir to incorporate.

2. Place the filling in the crust and use a rubber spatula to distribute it evenly. Place the pie in the refrigerator and chill it for at least 2 hours.

3. Slice and serve the pie, topping each slice with strawberries, if desired.

Lemon Tart

Yield: 1 Tart ◆ Active Time: 30 Minutes ◆ Total Time: 1 Hour and 30 Minutes

¾ cup fresh lemon juice

4 eggs

¾ cup sugar

⅛ teaspoon kosher salt

¼ teaspoon pure vanilla extract

½ cup unsalted butter, softened

1 Pâte Sucrée (see page 277), blind baked in a 9-inch tart pan

Fresh fruit, for topping

1. Fill a small saucepan halfway with water and bring it to a gentle simmer.

2. Place the lemon juice in a small saucepan and warm it over low heat.

3. Combine the eggs, sugar, salt, and vanilla in a metal mixing bowl. Place the bowl over the simmering water and whisk the mixture continually until it is 135°F.

4. When the lemon juice comes to a simmer, gradually add it to the egg mixture while whisking constantly.

5. When all of the lemon juice has been incorporated, whisk the curd until it has thickened and is 155°F. Remove the bowl from heat, add the butter, and stir until thoroughly incorporated.

6. Transfer the curd to a mason jar, place plastic wrap directly on its surface, and let it cool.

7. Transfer the lemon curd to the crust and smooth the top with a rubber spatula. Top the tart with fresh fruit and serve.

Linzer Tart

Yield: 1 Tart   Active Time: 30 Minutes   Total Time: 2 Hours and 45 Minutes

3.3 oz. fine almond flour

7 oz. sugar

6 oz. unsalted butter, softened

1 teaspoon lemon zest

3 eggs

5.3 oz. all-purpose flour, plus more as needed

½ teaspoon cinnamon

¼ teaspoon ground cloves

1 tablespoon unsweetened cocoa powder

¼ teaspoon kosher salt

1½ cups raspberry jam

1. Preheat the oven to 250°F. Place the almond flour on a baking sheet, place it in the oven, and toast for 5 minutes. Remove the almond flour from the oven and set it aside.

2. In the work bowl of a stand mixer fitted with the paddle attachment, combine the sugar, butter, and lemon zest and beat on medium until the mixture is pale and fluffy.

3. Incorporate two of the eggs one at a time, scraping down the work bowl as needed.

4. Place the flour, almond flour, cinnamon, cloves, cocoa powder, and salt in a separate bowl and whisk to combine. Gradually add this mixture to the wet mixture and beat until the resulting mixture comes together as a dough. Divide the dough in half, cover each piece with plastic wrap, and refrigerate it for 1 hour.

5. Preheat the oven to 350°F and coat a 9-inch tart pan with nonstick cooking spray. Place the pieces of dough on a flour-dusted work surface and roll them out to fit the tart pan. Place one piece of dough in the pan and then cut the other piece of dough into ¾-inch-wide strips.

6. Fill the crust in the pan with the jam. Lay some of the strips over the tart and trim any excess. To make a lattice crust, lift every other strip and fold back so you can place another strip across those strips that remain flat. Lay the folded strips back down over the cross-strip. Fold back the strips that you laid the cross-strip on top of and repeat until the lattice covers the surface of the tart. Beat the remaining egg until scrambled and brush the strips with it, taking care not to get any egg on the filling.

7. Place the tart in the oven and bake for about 45 minutes, until the lattice crust is golden brown. Remove the tart from the oven and let it cool before serving.

Pumpkin Pie

Yield: 1 Pie ◇ Active Time: 30 Minutes ◇ Total Time: 5 Hours

- 1 (14 oz.) can of pumpkin puree
- 1 (12 oz.) can of evaporated milk
- 2 eggs
- 6 oz. light brown sugar
- 1 teaspoon cinnamon
- 1 teaspoon ground ginger
- ½ teaspoon freshly grated nutmeg
- ¼ teaspoon ground cloves
- ½ teaspoon kosher salt
- 1 Perfect Piecrust (see page 276), blind baked
- Whipped Cream (see page 267), for serving

1 Preheat the oven to 350°F. In a mixing bowl, whisk together the pumpkin puree, evaporated milk, eggs, brown sugar, cinnamon, ginger, nutmeg, cloves, and salt. When the mixture is smooth, pour it into the crust.

2 Place the pie in the oven and bake until the filling is just set, about 40 minutes. Remove from the oven and let the pie cool at room temperature for 30 minutes before transferring it to the refrigerator. Chill the pie for 3 hours.

3 Slice the pie, top each piece with a dollop of Whipped Cream, and serve.

Sweet Potato Pie

Yield: 1 Pie ⋄ Active Time: 20 Minutes ⋄ Total Time: 4 Hours and 30 Minutes

15 oz. sweet potato puree

2 eggs

½ cup heavy cream

1 cup dark brown sugar

1 teaspoon cinnamon

½ teaspoon freshly grated nutmeg

¼ teaspoon ground ginger

½ teaspoon pure vanilla extract

¼ teaspoon kosher salt

1 Perfect Piecrust (see page 276)

Whipped Cream (see page 267), for serving

1. Preheat the oven to 350°F. Place the sweet potato puree, eggs, heavy cream, brown sugar, cinnamon, nutmeg, ginger, vanilla, and salt in a mixing bowl and whisk until smooth.

2. Pour the filling into the crust, place the pie in the oven, and bake until the filling is just set, about 30 minutes.

3. Remove the pie from the oven, place it on a cooling rack, and let it sit for 30 minutes.

4. Place the pie in the refrigerator and chill for 3 hours.

5. To serve, top each slice with a dollop of Whipped Cream.

Saltine Toffee, see page 259

Custards
& Other Decadent Confections

With all of the baking you'll end up doing around the holidays, it is important to find recipes that can make the most of everything you've purchased and prepared—a preparation that calls for just a few eggs, a dish that can use up the end of the sourdough loaf you made for the big breakfast on Christmas morning.

Many of these recipes will help you meet this call, while providing yet another decadent treat or two to add to the dessert table. Compared to the rest of the book, the recipes in this chapter are simple and straightforward. But they are also so delicious that they carry the ability to make one realize how little one needs to actually be happy—always a good thing to keep in mind around the holidays.

Eggnog Crème Brûlée

Yield: 6 Servings ◆ Active Time: 30 Minutes ◆ Total Time: 3 Hours and 30 Minutes

6 eggs, separated

4 cups heavy cream

Seeds and pod of 1 vanilla bean

2 tablespoons freshly grated nutmeg, or to taste

2 tablespoons cinnamon

1 tablespoon ground ginger, or to taste

¾ cup sugar

1. Preheat the oven to 325°F. Place the egg whites in the work bowl of a stand mixer fitted with the paddle attachment and whip until they hold soft peaks. Chill the whipped egg whites in the refrigerator.

2. Place the cream and vanilla seeds and pod in a saucepan and bring to a simmer over medium-high heat. Remove from heat, stir in the nutmeg, cinnamon, and ginger, cover the pan, and let the mixture steep for 15 minutes.

3. Remove the vanilla bean pod and discard it. Place ½ cup of sugar and the egg yolks in a mixing bowl and whisk until combined. While whisking continually, add the cream mixture in ¼-cup increments. Add the egg whites and fold to incorporate.

4. Divide the mixture among six 8 oz. ramekins. Transfer the ramekins to a 13 x 9-inch baking pan. Add hot water (about 125°F) until it reaches halfway up the sides of the ramekins, place the dish in the oven, and bake until the custard is just set, about 40 minutes.

5. Remove the ramekins from the oven, transfer them to the refrigerator, and chill for 2 hours.

6. Remove the ramekins 30 minutes before you are ready to serve them and let the custard to come to room temperature.

7. Divide the remaining sugar between the ramekins and spread it evenly over the top. Use a kitchen torch to caramelize the sugar, let the crème brûlées sit for 5 minutes, and serve.

Bread Pudding

Yield: 16 Servings ◆ Active Time: 45 Minutes ◆ Total Time: 24 Hours

- 8 cups sourdough bread pieces
- 3 cups whole milk
- 3 tablespoons unsalted butter
- 2¼ cups sugar
- ¾ cup heavy cream
- 1½ teaspoons cinnamon
- ½ teaspoon freshly grated nutmeg
- ¼ teaspoon kosher salt
- 3 eggs
- 1½ teaspoons pure vanilla extract
- Confectioners' sugar, for dusting

1. Place the bread in a mixing bowl and let it rest overnight at room temperature, uncovered, to dry out.
2. Place the milk, butter, sugar, cream, cinnamon, nutmeg, and salt in a medium saucepan and bring the mixture to a simmer, stirring until the butter has melted. Remove the pan from heat and briefly set it aside.
3. Place the eggs and vanilla in a heatproof mixing bowl and whisk to combine. Whisking constantly, gradually add the milk mixture until all of it has been incorporated.
4. Coat a 13 x 9-inch baking pan with nonstick cooking spray and then distribute the bread pieces in it. Slowly pour the custard over the bread and gently shake the pan to ensure it is evenly distributed. Press down on the bread with a rubber spatula so it soaks up the custard. Cover the baking pan with aluminum foil, place it in the refrigerator, and chill for 2 hours.
5. Preheat the oven to 350°F.
6. Place the baking pan in the oven and bake for 45 minutes. Remove the aluminum foil and bake until the bread pudding is golden brown on top, about 15 minutes.
7. Remove from the oven and let the bread pudding cool slightly before sprinkling confectioners' sugar over the top, slicing, and serving.

Crema Catalana

Yield: 4 Servings ◆ Active Time: 30 Minutes ◆ Total Time: 6 Hours and 30 Minutes

8 egg yolks

1½ cups heavy cream

7 oz. milk

Seeds of ½ vanilla bean

7 oz. sugar

Zest of ½ orange

¼ teaspoon kosher salt

1. Place the egg yolks in a mixing bowl, whisk to combine, and set them aside.

2. Combine the heavy cream, milk, vanilla seeds, three-quarters of the sugar, the orange zest, and salt in a saucepan and bring the mixture to a simmer. Remove the pan from heat and strain the mixture into a clean bowl through a fine-mesh sieve.

3. Whisking constantly, gradually add the warm mixture to the egg yolk mixture. When all of the warm mixture has been incorporated, place the custard in the refrigerator and chill for 4 hours.

4. Preheat the oven to 325°F. Bring 8 cups of water to a boil and then set it aside.

5. Fill four 8 oz. ramekins three-quarters of the way with the custard.

6. Place the ramekins in a 13 x 9-inch baking pan and pour the boiling water into the pan until it reaches halfway up the sides of the ramekins. Place the pan in the oven and bake until the custards are set at their edges and jiggle slightly at their centers, about 50 minutes. Remove from the oven and carefully transfer the ramekins to a wire rack. Let cool for 1 hour.

7. Place the ramekins in the refrigerator and chill for 4 hours.

8. Divide the remaining sugar between the ramekins and spread it evenly on top. Use a kitchen torch to caramelize the sugar and serve.

CUSTARDS & OTHER DECADENT CONFECTIONS

Panna Cotta

Yield: 4 Servings ◇ Active Time: 30 Minutes ◇ Total Time: 4 Hours and 30 Minutes

3½ sheets of silver gelatin

13 oz. heavy cream

13 oz. milk

3½ oz. sugar

Seeds and pod of ½ vanilla bean

Caramel Sauce (see page 271), for topping

1. Place the gelatin sheets in a small bowl. Add 1 cup of ice and water until the sheets are submerged. Let the mixture rest.

2. Combine the heavy cream, milk, sugar, and the vanilla seeds and pod in a saucepan and bring to a simmer. Cook for 15 minutes and then remove the pan from heat. Remove the vanilla bean pod and discard it.

3. Remove the bloomed gelatin from the ice water. Squeeze to remove as much water from the sheets as possible, add them to the warm mixture, and whisk until they have completely dissolved.

4. Strain the mixture into a bowl through a fine-mesh sieve and divide it between four 8 oz. ramekins, leaving about ½ inch of space at the top. Carefully transfer the ramekins to the refrigerator and chill until the panna cottas are fully set, about 4 hours.

5. To serve, drizzle the Caramel Sauce over the top of the panna cottas.

Raspberry & Pomegranate Pavlova

Yield: 4 Servings ◆ Active Time: 30 Minutes ◆ Total Time: 2 Hours and 50 Minutes

4 egg whites, at room temperature

¼ teaspoon cream of tartar

1 cup sugar

1 teaspoon pure vanilla extract

1 cup fresh raspberries, for topping

½ cup pomegranate arils, for topping

¼ cup fresh mint, for topping

1. Preheat the oven to 250°F and line a baking sheet with parchment paper. Place the egg whites and cream of tartar in the work bowl of a stand mixer fitted with the whisk attachment and whip until the mixture is foamy, 2 to 3 minutes.

2. With the mixer running, add the sugar 1 tablespoon at a time and whip until the sugar has been incorporated and the mixture holds stiff peaks.

3. Add the vanilla and whip to incorporate. Spoon the meringue onto the baking sheet and use a rubber spatula to spread it into a large rectangle.

4. Place the meringue in the oven and bake until it is firm and dry to the touch, about 1 hour. Turn off the oven and let the meringue cool in the oven for 1 hour.

5. Remove the pan from the oven and let the pavlova cool completely.

6. Top the pavlova with the raspberries, pomegranate, and mint and serve.

Peppermint Meringues

Yield: 50 Kisses ◆ Active Time: 30 Minutes ◆ Total Time: 1 Hour and 30 Minutes

4 egg whites

1 cup sugar

Pinch of kosher salt

½ teaspoon peppermint extract

2 drops of red gel food coloring

1. Preheat the oven to 200°F and line two baking sheets with parchment paper.

2. Fill a small saucepan halfway with water and bring it to a gentle simmer. In the work bowl of a stand mixer, combine the egg whites, sugar, and salt. Place the work bowl over the simmering water and whisk continually until the sugar has dissolved. Remove the bowl from heat and return it to the stand mixer.

3. Fit the mixer with the whisk attachment and whip the mixture on high speed until it holds stiff peaks. Add the peppermint extract and whisk to incorporate.

4. Add the food coloring and use a rubber spatula to just incorporate it, creating a swirled effect.

5. Transfer the meringue to a piping bag fit with a round tip.

6. Pipe the meringue onto the baking sheets, leaving about 1 inch between them. Place the sheets in the oven and bake the meringues until they can be pulled off the parchment cleanly and are no longer sticky in the center, about 1 hour. If the meringues need a little longer, crack the oven door and continue cooking. This will prevent the meringues from browning.

7. Remove the meringues from the oven and serve immediately.

Sticky Toffee Pudding

Yield: 8 Small Cakes ◆ Active Time: 45 Minutes ◆ Total Time: 1 Hour and 30 Minutes

¾ cup plus 1 tablespoon warm water (110°F)

½ teaspoon baking soda

8 oz. pitted dates, chopped

6¼ oz. all-purpose flour

½ teaspoon baking powder

¾ teaspoon fine sea salt

12¼ oz. dark brown sugar

2 large eggs

4 oz. unsalted butter, half melted, half softened

1½ tablespoons pure vanilla extract

1 cup heavy cream

Dash of fresh lemon juice

1. Place ¾ cup of warm water, the baking soda, and half of the dates in a large mason jar and let the dates soak for 5 minutes.

2. Preheat the oven to 350°F and coat eight 4 oz. ramekins with nonstick cooking spray. Bring water to boil in a small saucepan.

3. Place the flour, baking powder, and ½ teaspoon of the salt in a large bowl and whisk to combine.

4. Place ¾ cup of the brown sugar and the remaining dates in a blender or food processor and blitz until the mixture is fine. Drain the soaked dates, reserve the liquid, and set them aside. Add the reserved liquid to the blender with the eggs, melted butter, and vanilla and puree until smooth. Add the puree and soaked dates to the flour mixture and fold to combine.

5. Fill each ramekin two-thirds of the way with the batter, place the filled ramekins in a large roasting pan, and pour the boiling water in the roasting pan so that it goes halfway up each ramekin.

6. Cover tightly with aluminum foil and place the pan in the oven. Bake until each cake is puffy and the surfaces are spongy but firm, about 40 minutes. Remove the ramekins from the roasting pan and let them cool on a wire rack for 10 minutes.

7. Place the remaining butter in a saucepan and warm over medium-high heat. When the butter is melted, add the remaining brown sugar and salt and whisk until smooth. Cook, while stirring occasionally, until the brown sugar has dissolved. Slowly add the cream, while stirring constantly, until it has all been incorporated and the mixture is smooth. Reduce the heat to low and simmer until the mixture starts to bubble. Remove from heat and stir in the lemon juice.

8. To serve, invert each cake into a bowl or onto a dish, and spoon a generous amount of the sauce over each.

CUSTARDS & OTHER DECADENT CONFECTIONS

Flan

Yield: 6 Servings ◆ Active Time: 30 Minutes ◆ Total Time: 6 Hours and 30 Minutes

2 cups sugar

¼ cup water

5 egg yolks

5 eggs

5 oz. cream cheese, softened

1 (14 oz.) can of sweetened condensed milk

1 (12 oz.) can of evaporated milk

1½ cups heavy cream

½ teaspoon almond extract

½ teaspoon pure vanilla extract

1. Preheat the oven to 350°F. Bring 2 quarts of water to a boil and set it aside.

2. Place 1 cup of the sugar and the water in a small saucepan and bring to a boil over high heat, swirling the pan instead of stirring. Cook until the caramel is a deep golden brown, taking care not to burn it. Remove the pan from heat and pour the caramel into a round 8-inch cake pan. Place the cake pan on a cooling rack and let it sit until it has set.

3. Place the egg yolks, eggs, cream cheese, remaining sugar, condensed milk, evaporated milk, heavy cream, almond extract, and vanilla in a blender and puree until emulsified.

4. Pour the mixture over the caramel and place the cake pan in a roasting pan. Pour the boiling water into the roasting pan until it reaches halfway up the side of the cake pan.

5. Place the flan in the oven and bake until it is just set, 60 to 70 minutes. The flan should still be jiggly without being runny. Remove from the oven, place the cake pan on a cooling rack, and let it cool for 1 hour.

6. Place the flan in the refrigerator and chill for 4 hours.

7. Run a knife along the edge of the pan and invert the flan onto a plate so that the caramel layer is on top. Slice the flan and serve.

Macadamia Brittle

Yield: 24 Servings ◇ Active Time: 40 Minutes ◇ Total Time: 2 Hours and 30 Minutes

- 1½ cups macadamia nuts
- 1 tablespoon unsalted butter, softened
- ½ cup light corn syrup
- 3½ oz. brown sugar
- 1 lb. sugar
- ½ teaspoon kosher salt
- ½ cup water
- ½ teaspoon pure vanilla extract
- ¾ teaspoon baking soda

1. Preheat the oven to 350°F. Line a baking sheet with parchment paper and place the macadamia nuts on it. Place in the oven and roast until golden brown and fragrant, about 15 minutes. Remove the nuts from the oven and let them cool for 30 minutes.

2. Place the nuts in a food processor and pulse until roughly chopped.

3. Make sure all of the ingredients are measured out, as you must work quickly once the sugar caramelizes. Place two 18 x 13-inch silicone mats on the counter, along with one rolling pin and a cooling rack.

4. In a large saucepan fitted with a candy thermometer, combine the butter, corn syrup, brown sugar, sugar, and salt and cook over medium heat, swirling the pan occasionally, until the caramel reaches 248°F.

5. Remove the pan from heat and carefully whisk in the water and vanilla.

6. Add the baking soda and toasted macadamia nuts and work quickly, whisking the mixture to deflate the bubbling up of the caramel.

7. Pour the mixture over one of the mats, using a rubber spatula to remove all of the caramel from the pan. Place the second mat on top. Using the rolling pin, roll the caramel out until it is the length and width of the mats.

8. Carefully transfer the mats to the cooling rack. Allow the brittle to set for at least an hour before breaking it up.

Saltine Toffee

Yield: 20 Pieces ◆ Active Time: 35 Minutes ◆ Total Time: 2 Hours and 15 Minutes

40 saltines

1 cup unsalted butter, cubed

1 cup brown sugar

¾ lb. chocolate chips or chocolate melting wafers

1 cup English toffee pieces

½ cup chopped pecans

1 Preheat the oven to 350°F. Line a 15 x 10-inch rimmed baking sheet with aluminum foil. Arrange the saltines on the baking sheet in a single layer.

2 In a heavy saucepan, melt the butter. Stir in the brown sugar and bring the mixture to a boil. Cook, stirring continually, until the sugar has dissolved, 1 to 2 minutes.

3 Pour the mixture evenly over the crackers. Place the baking sheet in the oven and bake until the topping is bubbly, about 6 minutes.

4 While the saltines are in the oven, place the chocolate in a microwave-safe bowl and microwave for 1 minute. Remove the bowl from the microwave, stir, and then microwave in 15-second intervals until the chocolate is almost melted, stirring after each interval. Remove the chocolate from the microwave and stir until it is smooth.

5 Remove the baking sheet from the oven and carefully spread the melted chocolate over the mixture. Sprinkle the toffee and pecans over the chocolate and let the saltine toffee cool completely.

6 Cover the saltine toffee with plastic wrap and chill it in the refrigerator until set, about 1 hour.

7 Break the toffee into pieces and serve.

Nougat

Yield: 24 Servings ◆ **Active Time: 30 Minutes** ◆ **Total Time: 1 Hour and 30 Minutes**

3 large egg whites

3 cups sugar

⅓ cup light corn syrup

1 cup honey

1 cup water

Zest of 1 lemon

Seeds of 2 vanilla beans

¾ teaspoon fine sea salt

½ cup sliced almonds, toasted

½ cup pistachios, chopped

¼ cup dried cranberries, chopped

1. Coat a rimmed baking sheet with nonstick cooking spray. Place the egg whites in the work bowl of a stand mixer fitted with the whisk attachment and beat until frothy. Set aside.

2. Place the sugar, corn syrup, honey, and water in a saucepan fitted with a candy thermometer and bring to a boil over medium-high heat. Cook until the mixture is 300°F.

3. With the mixer running on low, gradually add the hot syrup to the egg whites. When half of the syrup has been incorporated, pour the rest of the hot syrup into the mixture and gradually increase the speed until the mixture is light and frothy. Add the lemon zest, vanilla seeds, salt, almonds, pistachios, and cranberries and continue to run the mixer until the mixture has cooled considerably, about 15 to 20 minutes.

4. Pour the mixture onto the baking sheet and let it cool completely before slicing into bars, about 1 hour.

CUSTARDS & OTHER DECADENT CONFECTIONS

Appendix

Royal Icing

Yield: 3 Cups ✧ Active Time: 5 Minutes ✧ Total Time: 5 Minutes

6 egg whites

1 teaspoon pure vanilla extract

2 lbs. confectioners' sugar

2 drops of gel food coloring (optional)

1. Place the egg whites, vanilla, and confectioners' sugar in a mixing bowl and whisk until the mixture is smooth.
2. If desired, add the food coloring. If using immediately, place the icing in a piping bag. If making ahead of time, store in the refrigerator, where it will keep for 5 days.

Butterfluff Filling

Yield: 4 Cups ✧ Active Time: 10 Minutes ✧ Total Time: 10 Minutes

½ lb. marshmallow creme

10 oz. unsalted butter, softened

11 oz. confectioners' sugar

1½ teaspoons pure vanilla extract

¾ teaspoon kosher salt

1. In the work bowl of a stand mixer fitted with the paddle attachment, cream the marshmallow creme and butter on medium speed until the mixture is light and fluffy, about 5 minutes.
2. Add the confectioners' sugar, vanilla, and salt, reduce the speed to low, and beat for 2 minutes. Use immediately, or store in the refrigerator for up to 1 month.

Vanilla Glaze

Yield: 1½ Cups ◆ Active Time: 5 Minutes ◆ Total Time: 5 Minutes

½ cup milk, plus more as needed

¼ teaspoon pure vanilla extract

1 lb. confectioners' sugar, plus more as needed

1. In a mixing bowl, whisk all of the ingredients until combined.
2. If the glaze is too thick, incorporate tablespoons of milk until it reaches the desired consistency. If it is too thin, incorporate tablespoons of confectioners' sugar. Use immediately, or store in the refrigerator for up to 5 days.

American Buttercream

Yield: 3 Cups ◆ Active Time: 10 Minutes ◆ Total Time: 10 Minutes

1 lb. unsalted butter, softened

2 lbs. confectioners' sugar

⅛ teaspoon kosher salt

¼ cup heavy cream

½ teaspoon pure vanilla extract

1. In the work bowl of a stand mixer fitted with the paddle attachment, combine the butter, confectioners' sugar, and salt and beat on low speed until the sugar starts to be incorporated into the butter. Raise the speed to high and beat until the mixture is smooth and fluffy, about 5 minutes.
2. Reduce the speed to low, add the heavy cream and vanilla, and beat until incorporated. Use immediately, or store in the refrigerator for up to 2 weeks. If refrigerating, return to room temperature before using.

Chocolate Ganache

Yield: 1½ Cups ◇ Active Time: 10 Minutes ◇ Total Time: 2 Hours and 30 Minutes

½ lb. chocolate (dark, milk, or white)

1 cup heavy cream

1. Place the chocolate in a heatproof mixing bowl and set it aside.

2. Place the heavy cream in a small saucepan and bring to a simmer over medium heat.

3. Pour the cream over the chocolate and let the mixture rest for 1 minute.

4. Gently whisk the mixture until thoroughly combined. Use immediately if drizzling over a cake or serving with fruit. Let the ganache cool for 2 hours if piping. The ganache will keep in the refrigerator for up to 5 days.

Pisto

Yield: ¼ Cup ◇ Active Time: 5 Minutes ◇ Total Time: 5 Minutes

4 teaspoons cinnamon

2 teaspoons coriander

2 teaspoons black pepper

2 teaspoons freshly grated nutmeg

1 teaspoon ground cloves

½ teaspoon ground star anise

1. Place all of the ingredients in a bowl, stir to combine, and use immediately or store in an airtight container.

Whipped Cream

Yield: 2 Cups ◆ Active Time: 5 Minutes ◆ Total Time: 5 Minutes

2 cups heavy cream

3 tablespoons sugar

1 teaspoon pure vanilla extract

1. In the work bowl of a stand mixer fitted with the whisk attachment, whip the heavy cream, sugar, and vanilla on high until the mixture holds soft peaks.

2. Use immediately, or store in the refrigerator for up to 3 days.

Classic Chocolate Frosting

Yield: 1½ Cups ◆ Active Time: 15 Minutes ◆ Total Time: 1 Hour and 30 Minutes

1 lb. milk chocolate, chopped

⅔ cup heavy cream

1 cup unsalted butter, divided into tablespoons and softened

1. Fill a small saucepan halfway with water and bring it to a simmer over medium heat.

2. Place the chocolate and cream in a large heatproof bowl and place it over the simmering water. Stir occasionally until the mixture is smooth and glossy.

3. Remove the bowl from heat, add the butter, and stir briefly. Let the mixture stand until the butter is melted, about 5 minutes, and then stir until the mixture is smooth.

4. Place the frosting in the refrigerator until it is cool and has thickened, 30 minutes to 1 hour.

Almond Syrup

Yield: ½ Cup ✧ Active Time: 10 Minutes ✧ Total Time: 1 Hour

½ cup water

½ cup sugar

¼ teaspoon almond extract

1. Place the water and sugar in a small saucepan and bring to a boil over medium heat, stirring to dissolve the sugar.

2. Remove the saucepan from heat, stir in the almond extract, and let the syrup cool completely before using or storing in the refrigerator.

Brown Butter

Yield: 1 Lb. ✧ Active Time: 10 Minutes ✧ Total Time: 10 Minutes

1½ lbs. unsalted butter

1. Place the butter in a large saucepan and melt it over medium heat, stirring frequently, until the butter starts to give off a nutty smell and turn golden brown (let your nose lead the way here, frequently wafting the steam toward you).

2. Remove the pan from heat and strain the butter through a fine sieve. Let the butter cool and solidify before using or storing in the refrigerator.

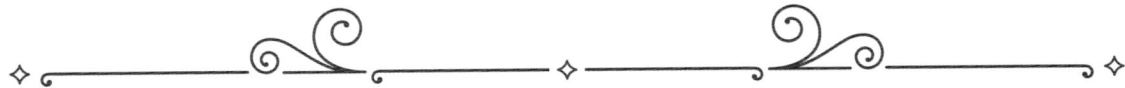

Caramelized White Chocolate

Yield: 1 Cup ✧ Active Time: 25 Minutes ✧ Total Time: 1 Hour and 30 Minutes

1 lb. white chocolate

Pinch of fine sea salt

2 tablespoons canola oil

1. Preheat the oven to 250°F.
2. Line a rimmed 18 x 13-inch baking sheet with a Silpat mat.
3. Chop the white chocolate into small pieces and spread them over the pan. Add the salt and oil and stir to coat the chocolate pieces.
4. Place the pan in the oven and bake for 10 minutes.
5. Use a rubber spatula to spread the chocolate until it covers the entire pan. Place back in the oven and bake until the white chocolate has caramelized to a deep golden brown, about 30 to 50 minutes, removing to stir every 10 minutes.
6. Carefully pour the caramelized white chocolate into a heat-proof container. Store at room temperature for up to 1 month.

Sourdough Starter

Yield: 2 Cups ◆ Active Time: 2 Hours ◆ Total Time: 2 Weeks

1 cup water, at room temperature, plus more daily

2 cups all-purpose flour, plus more daily

1. Place the water and flour in a large jar (the jar should be at least 1 quart). Combine the ingredients by hand, cover the jar, and let it stand in a sunny spot at room temperature for 24 hours.

2. Place 1 cup of the starter in a bowl, add 1 cup water and 2 cups all-purpose flour, and stir until thoroughly combined. Discard the remainder of the starter. Place the new mixture back in the jar and let it sit at room temperature for 24 hours. Repeat this process every day until you notice bubbles forming in the starter. This should take approximately 2 weeks.

3. Once the starter begins to bubble, it can be used in recipes. The starter can be stored at room temperature or in the refrigerator. If the starter is kept at room temperature it must be fed once a day; if the starter is refrigerated it can be fed every 3 days. The starter can be frozen for up to a month without feeding.

4. To feed the starter, place 1 cup of the starter in a bowl, add 1 cup flour and 1 cup water, and work the mixture with your hands until combined. Discard the remainder of the starter. It is recommended that you feed the starter 6 to 8 hours before making bread.

Caramel Sauce

Yield: 2 Cups ⋄ Active Time: 15 Minutes ⋄ Total Time: 1 Hour and 30 Minutes

1 cup sugar

¼ cup water

½ cup heavy cream

6 tablespoons unsalted butter, softened

½ teaspoon kosher salt

½ teaspoon pure vanilla extract

1. Place the sugar and water in a small saucepan and bring to a boil over high heat. Resist the urge to whisk the mixture; instead, swirl the pan occasionally.

2. Once the mixture turns a dark amber, turn off the heat and, whisking slowly, drizzle in the heavy cream. Be careful, as the mixture may splatter.

3. When all of the cream has been incorporated, add the butter, salt, and vanilla and whisk until smooth. Pour the hot caramel into a mason jar to cool. The caramel sauce can be stored for 1 week at room temperature.

Hazelnut Mousseline

Yield: 3 Cups ◆ Active Time: 20 Minutes ◆ Total Time: 2 Hours and 30 Minutes

½ cup sugar

6 egg yolks

3 tablespoons cornstarch

2 cups whole milk

¼ teaspoon kosher salt

1½ teaspoons pure vanilla extract

2 oz. unsalted butter, softened

¼ cup Hazelnut Praline Paste (see page 273)

1. Place the sugar, egg yolks, and cornstarch in a mixing bowl and whisk for 2 minutes, so that the mixture is thoroughly combined. Set it aside.

2. Place the milk in a medium saucepan and bring it to a simmer over medium heat. While whisking continually, gradually add the warm milk to the egg yolk mixture until it has all been incorporated.

3. Pour the tempered egg yolks into the saucepan and cook over medium heat, stirring constantly. When the custard has thickened and begins to simmer, cook for another 30 seconds and then remove the pan from heat.

4. Whisk in the remaining ingredients, strain the mousseline into a bowl through a fine-mesh sieve, and place plastic wrap directly on the top to keep a skin from forming. Place the mousseline in the refrigerator and chill for 2 hours before using. The mousseline will keep in the refrigerator for 5 days.

Hazelnut Praline Paste

Yield: 3 Cups ◆ Active Time: 25 Minutes ◆ Total Time: 2 Hours

2 cups hazelnuts

1 cup sugar

3 tablespoons water

2 teaspoons canola oil

¼ teaspoon fine sea salt

1. Place the hazelnuts in a large, dry skillet and toast over medium heat until they just start to brown, about 5 minutes. Transfer the nuts to a clean, dry kitchen towel, fold the towel over the nuts, and rub them together until the skins have loosened. Place the toasted nuts on a parchment-lined baking sheet and discard the skins.

2. Place the sugar and water in a small saucepan and warm the mixture over medium heat, swirling the pan occasionally instead of stirring the mixture. Cook until the mixture is a deep golden brown and then pour it over the toasted hazelnuts. Let the mixture sit at room temperature until it has set.

3. Break the hazelnut brittle into pieces, place them in a blender, and add the canola oil and salt. Puree until the mixture is a smooth paste and use immediately or store in the refrigerator.

Danish Dough

Yield: Dough for 20 Danishes ◆ Active Time: 2 Hours ◆ Total Time: 12 Hours

For the Dough

11 oz. milk

1 tablespoon active dry yeast

2 eggs

2 oz. sugar

22 oz. all-purpose flour, plus more as needed

1 tablespoon kosher salt

For the Butter Block

1 lb. unsalted butter, softened

¼ cup all-purpose flour

1. To begin preparations for the dough, place the milk and yeast in the work bowl of a stand mixer fitted with the dough hook, gently stir, and let the mixture sit until it starts to foam, about 10 minutes.

2. Add the eggs, sugar, flour, and salt and knead the mixture on low until it comes together as a smooth dough, about 5 minutes.

3. Spray a mixing bowl with nonstick cooking spray. Transfer the dough to the bowl, cover it with plastic wrap, and chill it in the refrigerator for 3 hours.

4. While the dough is resting, prepare the butter block. Fit the stand mixer with the paddle attachment, add the butter and flour, and beat the mixture until smooth. Transfer the mixture to a Silpat mat that is in a baking sheet. Use a small spatula to spread the mixture into a 7 x 10-inch rectangle. Place the baking sheet in the refrigerator for 30 minutes to 1 hour. You want the butter block to be firm but pliable. If the butter block is too firm for the following steps, let the butter sit at room temperature for a few minutes.

5. Remove the dough from the refrigerator, place it on a flour-dusted work surface, and roll it into a 10 x 20-inch rectangle.

6. Place the butter block in the center of the dough. Fold the dough over the butter block like a letter, folding a third of the dough from the left side of the dough and a third from the right so that they meet in the center. Pinch the seam to seal.

7. Turn the dough 90 degrees clockwise and flip it over so that the seam is facing down. Roll out the dough into a 10 x 20-inch rectangle. Make another letter fold of the dough, place the dough on the Silpat mat, and cover it with plastic wrap. Chill it in the refrigerator for 1 hour.

8. Place the dough on a flour-dusted work surface, roll it into a 10 x 20-inch rectangle, and fold the dough like a letter, lengthwise. Pinch the seam to seal, turn the dough 90 degrees clockwise, and flip the dough over so that the seam is facing down. Place the dough back on the baking sheet, cover it in plastic wrap, and refrigerate for 1 hour.

9. Place the dough on a flour-dusted work surface, roll it into a 10 x 20-inch rectangle, and fold the dough like a letter, lengthwise. Pinch the seam to seal, turn the dough 90 degrees clockwise, and flip the dough over so that the seam is facing down. Place the dough back on the baking sheet, cover it in plastic wrap, and refrigerate for 4 hours. After this period of rest, the dough will be ready to make danish with.

Perfect Piecrusts

Yield: 2 (9-Inch) Piecrusts ◇ Active Time: 15 Minutes ◇ Total Time: 2 Hours and 15 Minutes

1 cup unsalted butter, cubed

12½ oz. all-purpose flour, plus more as needed

½ teaspoon kosher salt

4 teaspoons sugar

½ cup ice water

1. Place the butter in a small bowl and place it in the freezer.
2. Place the flour, salt, and sugar in a food processor and pulse a few times until combined.
3. Add the chilled butter and pulse until the mixture is crumbly, consisting of pea-sized clumps.
4. Add the water and pulse until the mixture comes together as a dough.
5. Place the dough on a flour-dusted work surface and fold it over itself until it is a ball. Divide the dough in two and flatten each piece into a 1-inch-thick disc. Envelop each piece in plastic wrap and place in the refrigerator for at least 2 hours before rolling out to fit your pie plate.

Pâté Sucrée

Yield: 2 (9-Inch) Crusts ❖ Active Time: 15 Minutes ❖ Total Time: 2 Hours and 15 Minutes

1 cup unsalted butter, softened

½ lb. sugar

¼ teaspoon kosher salt

1 egg

2 egg yolks

1 lb. all-purpose flour, plus more as needed

1. In the work bowl of a stand mixer fitted with the paddle attachment, cream the butter, sugar, and salt on medium speed until the mixture is creamy, light, and fluffy, about 5 minutes.

2. Add the egg and egg yolks and beat until incorporated. Add the flour and beat until the mixture comes together as a dough.

3. Place the dough on a flour-dusted work surface and fold it over itself until it is a ball. Divide the dough in two and flatten each piece into a 1-inch-thick disc. Envelop each piece in plastic wrap and place in the refrigerator for at least 2 hours before rolling out to fit your tart pan or pie plate.

Graham Cracker Crust

Yield: 1 (9-Inch) Crust ◊ Active Time: 10 Minutes ◊ Total Time: 1 Hour

1½ cups graham cracker crumbs

2 tablespoons sugar

1 tablespoon real maple syrup

3 oz. unsalted butter, melted

1. Preheat the oven to 375°F. Place the graham cracker crumbs and sugar in a large mixing bowl and stir to combine. Add the maple syrup and 5 tablespoons of the melted butter and stir until thoroughly combined.

2. Coat a 9-inch pie plate with the remaining butter. Pour the dough into the pie plate and gently press into shape. Line the crust with aluminum foil, fill it with uncooked rice, dried beans, or pie weights, and bake for about 10 minutes, until the crust is firm.

3. Remove from the oven, remove the parchment paper and weight, and allow the crust to cool completely before filling.

Gianduja Crémeux

Yield: 4 Cups ✧ Active Time: 30 Minutes ✧ Total Time: 24 Hours

2 sheets of silver gelatin

¾ lb. gianduja chocolate, chopped

¼ cup sugar

4 egg yolks

¾ cup milk

¾ cup heavy cream

1. Place the gelatin sheets in a small bowl and add 1 cup of ice and enough cold water that the sheets are completely covered. Set aside.

2. Place the chocolate in a heatproof mixing bowl.

3. Place half of sugar and the egg yolks in a small bowl and whisk for 2 minutes. Set the mixture aside.

4. In a small saucepan, combine the milk, heavy cream, and remaining sugar and bring to a simmer over medium heat.

5. Slowly pour half of the hot milk mixture into the egg mixture and stir until incorporated. Pour the tempered egg mixture into the saucepan. Cook, while stirring constantly, until the mixture thickens and is about to come to a full simmer (if you have an instant-read thermometer, 175°F). Remove the pan from heat.

6. Remove the bloomed gelatin from the ice water. Squeeze to remove as much water as possible from the sheets. Add the sheets to the hot milk mixture base and whisk until they have completely dissolved.

7. Pour the hot milk mixture over the chocolate and let the mixture sit for 1 minute. Whisk to combine, transfer to a heatproof container, and let it cool to room temperature.

8. Store in the refrigerator overnight before using.

CONVERSION TABLE

WEIGHTS

1 oz. = 28 grams
2 oz. = 57 grams
4 oz. (¼ lb.) = 113 grams
8 oz. (½ lb.) = 227 grams
16 oz. (1 lb.) = 454 grams

VOLUME MEASURES

⅛ teaspoon = 0.6 ml
¼ teaspoon = 1.23 ml
½ teaspoon = 2.5 ml
1 teaspoon = 5 ml
1 tablespoon (3 teaspoons) = ½ fluid oz. = 15 ml
2 tablespoons = 1 fluid oz. = 29.5 ml
¼ cup (4 tablespoons) = 2 fluid oz. = 59 ml
⅓ cup (5⅓ tablespoons) = 2.7 fluid oz. = 80 ml
½ cup (8 tablespoons) = 4 fluid oz. = 120 ml
⅔ cup (10⅔ tablespoons) = 5.4 fluid oz. = 160 ml
¾ cup (12 tablespoons) = 6 fluid oz. = 180 ml
1 cup (16 tablespoons) = 8 fluid oz. = 240 ml

TEMPERATURE EQUIVALENTS

°F	°C	Gas Mark
225	110	¼
250	130	½
275	140	1
300	150	2
325	170	3
350	180	4
375	190	5
400	200	6
425	220	7
450	230	8
475	240	9
500	250	10

LENGTH MEASURES

¹⁄₁₆ inch = 1.6 mm
⅛ inch = 3 mm
¼ inch = 6.35 mm
½ inch = 1.25 cm
¾ inch = 2 cm
1 inch = 2.5 cm

INDEX

acorn squash
    Squash Whoopie Pies, 225
Alfajores, 58
almond flour/meal
    Chocolate-Dipped Orange Cookies, 82
    Kipferl Biscuits, 50
    Kourabiedes, 61
    Linzer Tart, 236
    Macarons, 42–43
    Madeleines, 34
    Opera Torte, 138–139
    Pepparkakor, 38
    Ricciarelli, 101
almond paste
    Gluten-Free Almond Torte, 119
    Pignoli, 27
Almond Syrup
    Gluten-Free Almond Torte, 119
    recipe, 268
almonds
    Amaretti Cookies, 74
    Baklava, 208
    Challah, 156–157
    Cortaditos de Anís, 20
    Florentines, 46
    Gluten-Free Almond Torte, 119
    Lebkuchen, 37
    Nougat, 261
    Nutty Caramel & Cranberry Pie, 224
    Paris-Brest, 199
    Polvorones, 16
    Roccocò, 81
    Stollen, 148–149
almonds, candied
    Gingerbread Muffins, 152
Amaretti Cookies, 74
American Buttercream
    Brown Butter Cake, 135
    Brownies from Scratch, 49
    Chocolate Beet Cake, 127
    Coconut Cake, 124–125
    Eggnog Cupcakes, 104
    Gluten-Free Vanilla Cake with Orange Marmalade & Cranberry Jam, 112–113
    recipe, 265
anise liqueur
    Cortaditos de Anís, 20

    Struffoli, 184
apples
    Apple Pie, 214
    Apple Strudel, 183
    Tarte Tatin, 228
apricots, dried
    Apricot Kolaches, 32

Baklava, 208
barley malt
    Pannettone, 172–173
Baumkuchen, 108
Beet Cake, Chocolate, 127
Beigli, 187
Black Forest Cake, 123
Bolo Rei, 128
Bread Pudding, 244
breads
    Beigli, 187
    Bread Pudding, 244
    Challah, 156–157
    Cinnamon Babka, 178–179
    Cinnamon Buns, 164–165
    Classic Gingerbread, 145
    Harvest Sourdough Bread, 146–147
    Holiday Brioche, 160–161
    Pumpkin Sticky Buns, 166–167
    Sourdough Bread, 169
    Stollen, 148–149
    Stout Gingerbread, 155
    Winter Harvest Loaf, 162–163
Brittle, Macadamia, 258
Brown Butter
    Brown Butter Cake, 135
    recipe, 268
Brownies from Scratch, 49
Brûléed Buttermilk Pie, 231
Butterfluff Filling
    Chocolate Yule Log, 106–107
    recipe, 264
    White Christmas Sandwich Cookies, 15
buttermilk
    Brûléed Buttermilk Pie, 231
    Gianduja Whoopie Pies, 218
    Gluten-Free Vanilla Cake with Orange Marmalade & Cranberry Jam, 112–113
    Red Velvet Cupcakes, 111
    Spice Cake, 136

butternut squash
    Squash Whoopie Pies, 225

cakes
    Baumkuchen, 108
    Black Forest Cake, 123
    Brown Butter Cake, 135
    Chocolate & Orange Financiers, 132
    Chocolate Beet Cake, 127
    Chocolate Cupcakes, 115
    Chocolate Yule Log, 106–107
    Coconut Cake, 124–125
    Eggnog Cupcakes, 104
    Flourless Chocolate Torte, 140
    Gluten-Free Almond Torte, 119
    Gluten-Free Vanilla Cake with Orange Marmalade & Cranberry Jam, 112–113
    Lamingtons, 131
    Opera Torte, 138–139
    Orange & Cardamom Cake, 120
    Red Velvet Cupcakes, 111
    Spice Cake, 136
Canelés, 194–195
Caramel Sauce
    Churros, 207
    Cinnamon Twists, 192
    Panna Cotta, 248
    recipe, 271
Caramelized White Chocolate
    Brown Butter Cake, 135
    recipe, 269
caraway seeds
    Winter Harvest Loaf, 162–163
cashews
    Nutty Caramel & Cranberry Pie, 224
Challah, 156–157
cherries, dried
    Florentines, 46
    Stollen, 148–149
cherry jam
    Black Forest Cake, 123
    Fiori di Mandilore, 54
Chewy Ginger Cookies, 19
chia seeds
    Harvest Sourdough Bread, 146–147
chocolate
    Baumkuchen, 108
    Chocolate Ganache, 266

Peanut Butter Blossoms, 90
Saltine Toffee, 259
chocolate, bittersweet
    Chocolate Truffle Pie, 232
chocolate, dark
    Brownies from Scratch, 49
    Chocolate & Peppermint Cookies, 57
    Chocolate Babka, 170-171
    Chocolate Beet Cake, 127
    Chocolate Crinkle Cookies, 70
    Chocolate Souffles, 116
    Chocolate-Dipped Orange Cookies, 82
    Florentines, 46
    Flourless Chocolate Torte, 140
    Lamingtons, 131
    Opera Torte, 138-139
    Peppermint Bars, 89
chocolate, gianduja
    Gianduja Crémeux, 279
chocolate, milk
    Chocolate & Peppermint Cookies, 57
    Classic Chocolate Frosting, 267
Chocolate, Peanut Butter & Raspberry Curls, 69
chocolate, semisweet
    Chocolate Chip Cookies, 66
    Chocolate-Dipped Sugar Cookies, 84-85
    Cranberry, Pumpkin Seed & Chocolate Chip Cookies, 93
    Lebkuchen, 37
chocolate, white
    Caramelized White Chocolate, 269
    Kipferl Biscuits, 50
    White Christmas Sandwich Cookies, 15
Chocolate Cupcakes, 115
Chocolate Ganache
    Chocolate & Orange Financiers, 132
    Chocolate & Peppermint Cookies, 57
    Chocolate Yule Log, 106-107
    Churros, 207
    Cookies 'N' Cream Tart, 220-221
    Opera Torte, 138-139
    Peppermint Bars, 89
    recipe, 266
    Stout Gingerbread, 155
Churros, 207
Cinnamon Babka, 178-179
Cinnamon Buns, 164-165
Cinnamon Twists, 192

citrus peels, candied
    Florentines, 46
    Pannettone, 172-173
    Stollen, 148-149
Classic Chocolate Frosting
    Chocolate Cupcakes, 115
    recipe, 267
Classic Gingerbread, 145
Classic Gingerbread Cookies, 12
Classic Sugar Cookies, 98
clementine zest
    Roccocò, 81
cocoa powder
    Black Forest Cake, 123
    Brownies from Scratch, 49
    Chocolate, Peanut Butter & Raspberry Curls, 69
    Chocolate & Peppermint Cookies, 57
    Chocolate Babka, 170-171
    Chocolate Beet Cake, 127
    Chocolate Crinkle Cookies, 70
    Chocolate Cupcakes, 115
    Chocolate Yule Log, 106-107
    Gianduja Whoopie Pies, 218
    Kipferl Biscuits, 50
    Lebkuchen, 37
    Linzer Tart, 236
    Peppermint Bars, 89
    Red Velvet Crinkle Cookies, 73
    Red Velvet Cupcakes, 111
    Roccocò, 81
    White Christmas Sandwich Cookies, 15
    Winter Harvest Loaf, 162-163
coconut
    Alfajores, 58
    Coconut Cake, 124-125
    Coconut Macaroons, 53
    Lamingtons, 131
    Snowballs, 77
coconut milk
    Coconut Cake, 124-125
coffee. see also espresso powder/ ground espresso
    Black Forest Cake, 123
    Chocolate Cupcakes, 115
Cognac
    Canelés, 194-195
conversion table, 282
cookies
    Alfajores, 58
    Amaretti Cookies, 74
    Apricot Kolaches, 32
    Brownies from Scratch, 49

Chewy Ginger Cookies, 19
Chocolate, Peanut Butter & Raspberry Curls, 69
Chocolate Chip Cookies, 66
Chocolate Crinkle Cookies, 70
Chocolate-Dipped Sugar Cookies, 84-85
Classic Gingerbread Cookies, 12
Classic Sugar Cookies, 98
Coconut Macaroons, 53
Cortaditos de Anís, 20
Cranberry, Orange & Pistachio Biscotti, 23
Cranberry, Pumpkin Seed & Chocolate Chip Cookies, 93
Fiori di Mandilore, 54
Florentines, 46
Gingerbread Madeleines, 78
Goro Cookies, 65
Kipferl Biscuits, 50
Lebkuchen, 37
Madeleines, 34
Orange Spritz, 31
Peanut Butter Blossoms, 90
Pepparkakor, 38
Peppermint Bars, 89
Pfeffernüsse, 62
Pignoli, 27
Pizzelles, 86
Polvorones, 16
Pumpkin Cheesecake Bars, 97
Red Velvet Crinkle Cookies, 73
Ricciarelli, 101
Roccocò, 81
Rugelach, 35
Snowballs, 77
Snowman Cookies, 24
Vanilla & Matcha Christmas Trees, 28
Vegan Ginger Molasses Cookies, 94
White Christmas Sandwich Cookies, 15
Cookies 'N' Cream Tart, 220-221
Cortaditos de Anís, 20
cranberries, dried
    Cranberry, Orange & Pistachio Biscotti, 23
    Harvest Sourdough Bread, 146-147
    Nougat, 261
cranberries, fresh
    Cranberry, Pumpkin Seed & Chocolate Chip Cookies, 93
    Cranberry Curd Pie, 227
    Nutty Caramel & Cranberry Pie, 224

cranberry jam
    Gluten-Free Vanilla Cake with
        Orange Marmalade & Cranberry
        Jam, 112–113
cream, heavy
    American Buttercream, 265
    Bread Pudding, 244
    Caramel Sauce, 271
    Chocolate Ganache, 266
    Chocolate Souffles, 116
    Chocolate Truffle Pie, 232
    Classic Chocolate Frosting, 267
    Crema Catalana, 247
    Flan, 256
    Gianduja Crémeux, 279
    Goro Cookies, 65
    Lemon & Ginger Scones, 174
    Panna Cotta, 248
    Peppermint Bars, 89
    Sticky Toffee Pudding, 255
    Sweet Potato Pie, 239
    Whipped Cream, 267
cream cheese
    Apricot Kolaches, 32
    Cookies 'N' Cream Tart, 220–221
    Eggnog Cupcakes, 104
    Flan, 256
    Lingonberry Cream Pie, 222
    Pumpkin Cheesecake Bars, 97
    Rugelach, 35
    Snowballs, 77
    Squash Whoopie Pies, 225
Crema Catalana, 247
Crème Brûlée, Eggnog, 243
crème de cacao
    Chocolate Truffle Pie, 232
crème fraiche
    Gingerbread Muffins, 152
custards and puddings
    Bread Pudding, 244
    Crema Catalana, 247
    Eggnog Crème Brûlée, 243
    Flan, 256
    Panna Cotta, 248
    Sticky Toffee Pudding, 255

Danish Dough
    Raspberry Danish, 200
    recipe, 274–275
dates
    Challah, 156–157
    Sticky Toffee Pudding, 255
dulce de leche
    Alfajores, 58

Eggnog Crème Brûlée, 243
Eggnog Cupcakes, 104
espresso powder/ground espresso. see
    also coffee
    Kipferl Biscuits, 50
    Opera Torte, 138–139
evaporated milk
    Flan, 256
    Pumpkin Pie, 238

fennel seeds
    Winter Harvest Loaf, 162–163
feuilletine flakes
    Opera Torte, 138–139
Fig & Pistachio Tart, 217
Fiori di Mandilore, 54
Flan, 256
Florentines, 46
Flores de Carnaval, 196
Flourless Chocolate Torte, 140
fruit, candied
    Bolo Rei, 128

Gianduja Crémeux
    Gianduja Whoopie Pies, 218
    recipe, 279
ginger, candied
    Stollen, 148–149
ginger, crystallized
    Lemon & Ginger Scones, 174
ginger, fresh
    Gingerbread Madeleines, 78
    Squash Whoopie Pies, 225
Ginger Cookies, Chewy, 19
Ginger Molasses Cookies, Vegan, 94
ginger snaps
    Lingonberry Cream Pie, 222
gingerbread
    Classic Gingerbread, 145
    Classic Gingerbread Cookies, 12
    Gingerbread Madeleines, 78
    Gingerbread Muffins, 152
    Stout Gingerbread, 155
Gluten-Free Almond Torte, 119
Gluten-Free Vanilla Cake with Orange
    Marmalade & Cranberry Jam, 112–113
Goro Cookies, 65
Graham Cracker Crust
    Cranberry Curd Pie, 227
    recipe, 278
graham crackers
    Pumpkin Cheesecake Bars, 97
Grand Marnier
    Stollen, 148–149

Harvest Sourdough Bread, 146–147
hazelnut flour
    Chocolate & Orange Financiers, 132
Hazelnut Mousseline
    Paris-Brest, 199
    recipe, 272
Hazelnut Praline Paste
    Hazelnut Mousseline, 272
    recipe, 273
hazelnuts
    Baklava, 208
    Hazelnut Praline Paste, 273
    Lebkuchen, 37
Holiday Brioche, 160–161
honey
    Baklava, 208
    Brûléed Buttermilk Pie, 231
    Holiday Brioche, 160–161
    Nougat, 261
    Pannettone, 172–173
    Struffoli, 184

Kipferl Biscuits, 50
Kourabiedes, 61

Lamingtons, 131
Lebkuchen, 37
lemon juice
    Apple Pie, 214
    Apple Strudel, 183
    Beigli, 187
    Brûléed Buttermilk Pie, 231
    Lemon Tart, 235
    Ricciarelli, 101
lemon zest
    Alfajores, 58
    Apple Pie, 214
    Apple Strudel, 183
    Beigli, 187
    Bolo Rei, 128
    Brûléed Buttermilk Pie, 231
    Flores de Carnaval, 196
    Lebkuchen, 37
    Lemon & Ginger Scones, 174
    Linzer Tart, 236
    Madeleines, 34
    Nougat, 261
    Pignoli, 27
    Roccocò, 81
    Stollen, 148–149
    Struffoli, 184
lemons
    Baklava, 208
lime juice/zest
    Snowballs, 77

Lingonberry Cream Pie, 222
Linzer Tart, 236

Macadamia Brittle, 258
Macarons, 42-43
Madeleines, 34
    Gingerbread, 78
Mantecados, 45
maple syrup
    Graham Cracker Crust, 278
    Squash Whoopie Pies, 225
marshmallow creme
    Butterfluff Filling, 264
marzipan
    Baumkuchen, 108
Matcha Christmas Trees, Vanilla &, 28
Meringues, Peppermint, 252
milk, powdered
    Pannettone, 172-173
millet seeds
    Winter Harvest Loaf, 162-163
mint
    Chocolate & Peppermint Cookies, 57
    Peppermint Bars, 89
    Peppermint Meringues, 252
    Raspberry & Pomegranate Pavlova, 251
molasses
    Chewy Ginger Cookies, 19
    Classic Gingerbread, 145
    Classic Gingerbread Cookies, 12
    Gingerbread Madeleines, 78
    Gingerbread Muffins, 152
    Pfeffernüsse, 62
    Stout Gingerbread, 155
    Vegan Ginger Molasses Cookies, 94
    Winter Harvest Loaf, 162-163
muffins
    Gingerbread Muffins, 152
    Orange Spice Muffins, 177

Nougat, 261
nuts. *see individual nut types*
Nutty Caramel & Cranberry Pie, 224

oats
    Winter Harvest Loaf, 162-163
olive oil
    Challah, 156
    Chocolate Babka, 170-171
    Cinnamon Babka, 178-179
    Cinnamon Buns, 164-165
    Mantecados, 45

Squash Whoopie Pies, 225
Struffoli, 184
Winter Harvest Loaf, 162-163
Opera Torte, 138-139
Orange & Cardamom Cake, 120
orange blossom water
    Bolo Rei, 128
    Kourabiedes, 61
orange juice
    Chocolate-Dipped Orange Cookies, 82
    Cranberry Curd Pie, 227
    Roccocò, 81
orange marmalade
    Gluten-Free Vanilla Cake with Orange Marmalade & Cranberry Jam, 112-113
orange peels, candied
    Pannettone, 172-173
    Roccocò, 81
Orange Spritz, 31
orange zest
    Chocolate & Orange Financiers, 132
    Chocolate-Dipped Orange Cookies, 82
    Cinnamon Babka, 178-179
    Cranberry, Orange & Pistachio Biscotti, 23
    Crema Catalana, 247
    Lebkuchen, 37
    Orange & Cardamom Cake, 120
    Orange Spice Muffins, 177
    Orange Spritz, 31
    Ricciarelli, 101
    Roccocò, 81
    Struffoli, 184
    Zeppole, 203
Oreos
    Cookies 'N' Cream Tart, 220-221
ouzo
    Kourabiedes, 61

Palmiers, 204
Panna Cotta, 248
Pannettone, 172-173
Paris-Brest, 199
pasta madre
    Pannettone, 172-173
pastries
    Apple Strudel, 183
    Baklava, 208
    Canelés, 194-195
    Churros, 207
    Cinnamon Twists, 192
    Flores de Carnaval, 196

Palmiers, 204
Paris-Brest, 199
Raspberry Danish, 200
Sopaipillas, 188
Struffoli, 184
Sufganiyot, 191
Zeppole, 203
Pâté Sucrée
    Fig & Pistachio Tart, 217
    Lemon Tart, 235
    recipe, 277
peanut butter
    Chocolate, Peanut Butter & Raspberry Curls, 69
    Peanut Butter Blossoms, 90
pecans
    Pecan Pie, 213
    Rugelach, 35
    Saltine Toffee, 259
Pepparkakor, 38
Peppermint Bars, 89
Peppermint Cookies, Chocolate &, 57
Peppermint Meringues, 252
Perfect Piecrust
    Apple Pie, 214
    Brûléed Buttermilk Pie, 231
    Chocolate Truffle Pie, 232
    Nutty Caramel & Cranberry Pie, 224
    Pecan Pie, 213
    Pumpkin Pie, 238
    recipe, 276
    Sweet Potato Pie, 239
Pfeffernüsse, 62
phyllo dough
    Apple Strudel, 183
    Baklava, 208
pies and tarts
    Apple Pie, 214
    Brûléed Buttermilk Pie, 231
    Chocolate Truffle Pie, 232
    Cookies 'N' Cream Tart, 220-221
    Cranberry Curd Pie, 227
    Fig & Pistachio Tart, 217
    Lemon Tart, 235
    Lingonberry Cream Pie, 222
    Linzer Tart, 236
    Nutty Caramel & Cranberry Pie, 224
    Pecan Pie, 213
    Pumpkin Pie, 238
    Sweet Potato Pie, 239
    Tarte Tatin, 228
Pignoli, 27
pine nuts

Pignoli, 27
pistachios
    Cranberry, Orange & Pistachio Biscotti, 23
    Fig & Pistachio Tart, 217
    Nougat, 261
Pisto
    recipe, 266
    Roccocò, 81
Pizzelles, 86
plums, dried
    Florentines, 46
Polvorones, 16
Pomegranate Pavlova, Raspberry &, 251
poppy seeds
    Beigli, 187
    Harvest Sourdough Bread, 146-147
praline paste
    Opera Torte, 138-139
puff pastry
    Cinnamon Twists, 192
    Palmiers, 204
pumpkin puree
    Pumpkin Cheesecake Bars, 97
    Pumpkin Pie, 238
    Pumpkin Sticky Buns, 166-167
    Spice Cake, 136
pumpkin seeds
    Cranberry, Pumpkin Seed & Chocolate Chip Cookies, 93
    Harvest Sourdough Bread, 146-147

raisins
    Beigli, 187
    Florentines, 46
    Pannettone, 172-173
    Stollen, 148-149
Raspberry & Pomegranate Pavlova, 251
raspberry jam
    Chocolate, Peanut Butter & Raspberry Curls, 69
    Coconut Cake, 124-125
    Linzer Tart, 236
    Raspberry Danish, 200
Red Velvet Crinkle Cookies, 73
Red Velvet Cupcakes, 111
Ricciarelli, 101
ricotta cheese
    Zeppole, 203
Roccocò, 81
Royal Icing
    Classic Gingerbread Cookies, 12
    Lemon & Ginger Scones, 174
    Pepparkakor, 38
    recipe, 264

Red Velvet Cupcakes, 111
Snowman Cookies, 24
Rugelach, 35
rum
    Canelés, 194-195
    Struffoli, 184

saffron
    Chocolate-Dipped Orange Cookies, 82
Saltine Toffee, 259
Sandwich Cookies, White Christmas, 15
Scones, Lemon & Ginger, 174
Snickerdoodles, 41
Snowballs, 77
Snowman Cookies, 24
Sopaipillas, 188
sour cream
    Black Forest Cake, 123
    Chocolate Cupcakes, 115
    Chocolate Souffles, 116
    Classic Gingerbread, 145
    Orange & Cardamom Cake, 120
    Orange Spice Muffins, 177
Sourdough Bread, 169
    Harvest, 146-147
Sourdough Starter
    Harvest Sourdough Bread, 146-147
    Pannettone, 172-173
    recipe, 270
    Sourdough Bread, 169
Spice Cake, 136
Squash Whoopie Pies, 225
Sticky Toffee Pudding, 255
Stollen, 148-149
Stout Gingerbread, 155
strawberries
    Chocolate Truffle Pie, 232
strawberry jam
    Sufganiyot, 191
Struffoli, 184
Sufganiyot, 191
sunflower seeds
    Harvest Sourdough Bread, 146-147
Sweet Potato Pie, 239
sweetened condensed milk
    Coconut Macaroons, 53
    Flan, 256
    Lingonberry Cream Pie, 222

Tarte Tatin, 228
tarts. see pies and tarts
Toffee, Saltine, 259
Toffee Pudding, Sticky, 255

Vanilla & Matcha Christmas Trees, 28
vanilla beans
    Canelés, 194-195
    Crema Catalana, 247
    Eggnog Crème Brûlée, 243
    Nougat, 261
    Panna Cotta, 248
    Pannettone, 172-173
    Ricciarelli, 101
    Stollen, 148-149
Vanilla Glaze
    Lebkuchen, 37
    Raspberry Danish, 200
    recipe, 265
    Vanilla & Matcha Christmas Trees, 28
Vegan Ginger Molasses Cookies, 94

walnuts
    Baklava, 208
    Chocolate-Dipped Sugar Cookies, 84-85
    Orange Spice Muffins, 177
Whipped Cream
    Black Forest Cake, 123
    Cranberry Curd Pie, 227
    Lingonberry Cream Pie, 222
    Pumpkin Cheesecake Bars, 97
    Pumpkin Pie, 238
    recipe, 267
    Sweet Potato Pie, 239
White Christmas Sandwich Cookies, 15
Whoopie Pies
    Gianduja, 218
    Squash, 225
Winter Harvest Loaf, 162-163

xanthan gum
    Gluten-Free Almond Torte, 119
    Gluten-Free Vanilla Cake with Orange Marmalade & Cranberry Jam, 112-113

Zeppole, 203

About Cider Mill Press Book Publishers

Good ideas ripen with time. From seed to harvest, Cider Mill Press brings fine reading, information, and entertainment together between the covers of its creatively crafted books. Our Cider Mill bears fruit twice a year, publishing a new crop of titles each spring and fall.

"Where Good Books Are Ready for Press"
501 Nelson Place
Nashville, Tennessee 37214

cidermillpress.com